Shakespeare
BY ANY OTHER NAME

Shakespeare
BY ANY OTHER NAME

Five Plays for Teenagers

Susan O'Connor

authorHOUSE®

AuthorHouse™ LLC
1663 Liberty Drive
Bloomington, IN 47403
www.authorhouse.com
Phone: 1-800-839-8640

Published by AuthorHouse   10/24/2013

ISBN: 978-1-4918-2027-8 (sc)
ISBN: 978-1-4918-2026-1 (e)

Library of Congress Control Number: 2013917277

Contents

For Marc, Dencil, and Sidney

Acknowledgments

My love for theatre and all of its components—acting, stage production, play writing—began when I was six years old and my first grade teacher cast me in the class play as a rabbit, one of the most unforgettable events of my life. Eight years later I took the stage again in Dencil Taylor's production of Synge's "Riders to the Sea." Soon afterward, completely enthralled with theatre life, such as it was for me in those days, I joined Marc Pettaway's Lake Charles Little Theatre's community, specifically the Saturday morning one designed for teenagers. When I heard about the auditions for *The Dark at the Top of the Stairs* by William Inge, I showed up, read, and got the part of Flirt Conroy. Life would never be the same. I was subsequently cast in one play or another every semester for the next eight years. When I became a teacher, I began directing and later writing plays rather than acting in them. Shakespeare ultimately became the standard bearer for theatre, and when I took an interest in verse speaking, it was University of Houston theatre director and founder of the Children's Theatre Festival and the Houston Shakespeare Festival Sidney Berger whose influence became invaluable in my own teaching of Shakespeare to secondary students. To all three of these mentors,

I owe much gratitude, not only for their knowledge and guidance but also for instilling in me the love I have today for every aspect of theatre, from acting and writing and directing to the pleasure of watching a story unfold on a stage.

Introduction

HOW IT ALL BEGAN

Each one of these plays for teenagers included in this book takes as its foundation—basically characters and plot—the comedies and romances of the inimitable William Shakespeare. So, if Shakespeare cannot be satisfactorily imitated, which is the widely accepted opinion of most scholars and teachers, why are so many of us attempting to do just that? The best answer I can offer, and it's only my personal excuse if one is needed, is that everything about Shakespeare's works—the wisdom, the humor, the heart-wrenching passion, the deeply human quality of his characters and the desires that motivate them, all wrapped up in exquisite verse and prose—makes us want to color everything we do in shades of Shakespeare. In short, spending time with Shakespeare, which includes imitating him, is possibly one of the greatest pastimes of my life. Besides, Shakespeare by any other name would seem as sweet and wonderful just because the plays have that familiar ring.

I have a shrine dedicated to Shakespeare in my classroom, odds and ends, from note pads and teapots to replicas of the buildings around Stratford and, yes, a Shakespeare action figure as well. Most are gifts from students over the number of years that I've been teaching Shakespeare. By the time I've shown the Trevor Nunn version of *Twelfth Night* and my middle school students have selected and memorized monologues from the eleven plays we've learned about, many of them are hooked. They, too, actually think studying about Shakespeare, the man and his plays and sonnets, is fun, and that's really the goal: to introduce Shakespeare in a way that not only prevents students from being afraid of him, but also creates a lifelong appreciation for his writing.

Because middle school students think about food an exorbitant amount of the day, I shamelessly use it as bait. We celebrate the holiday of Twelfth Night to understand why Shakespeare chose this title for his play. Parents use traditional recipes from *Dance of Language* for Twelfth cake and wassail, on which students feast for the two day celebration. Musicians who specialize in early music from nearby universities arrive that morning, set up, and entertain students between performances of well known monologues from the plays and recitations of the sonnets. Seventh and eighth graders who have learned to play this sixteenth century music sometimes join in. The excitement and sense of accomplishment contribute to not only a memorable experience but also a strong positive connection to studying Shakespeare. Students get the picture: No amount of planning and organization can convince them that this departure from a regular routine day isn't a bit zany, just like Twelfth Night itself.

Currently the latest Hollywood spin-off on Shakespeare is *She's the Man*, based on *Twelfth Night*. One play in this book, "Circle Dance," was written and produced with middle school students several months before the box office attraction appeared. Now, years later, my students are still watching and loving the film, delighted that they can make a modern relevant connection to the play we will study. Each year afterward, another play was written and produced, three by the youth theatre director of the local theatre in Houston,

Texas. Students who saw or performed in the plays were more likely to read the actual play by Shakespeare. True to the research, students will often read what they see. One student in particular, who had been in my class four years ago, just returned from studying Shakespeare with a tutor at Oxford and reminisced about the time she played the stepmother in "Imogen's War," the alter ego of *Cymbeline* in this collection. What great memories we have—the success, the laughs, the challenging costumes and set, the plot that will forever maintain Shakespeare's throne as monarch supreme of literature.

Several years ago I inherited a treasure from my mother's cousin, her scrapbook of World War I, which she compiled as a school project between 1915 and 1918. After spending some time reading through her own handwritten accounts as well as the articles, ads, and brochures she included, I knew I would use her research to write another play, one set during this particular war. Even though *Cymbeline* takes place during Roman Britain times, the universality of Shakespeare's play facilitated a good adaptation to WWI, and "Imogen's War," set in England and France near the end of the war, was conceived.

One of the world's favorite comedies, *As You Like It*, serves as the skeletal framework of "Games." The setting and plot have close ties: two fathers at odds with each other and their two daughters— cousins who are best friends—taking refuge at their lake house amidst a lovely forest. Enter the young man, whose brother has betrayed him, and he falls in love with one of the daughters. This play takes place in Texas, where the lakes and forests are plentiful, and the adaptation to Shakespeare works superbly because, well, it's the universality of the Bard once more. His plots work well almost anywhere.

Once a booming port city, Galveston Island off the coast of Texas is resplendent with Victorian culture. A hurricane at the turn of the century almost demolished it and certainly changed the path of population growth, but there remains a Victorian section of the city called The Strand, reminiscent of Dickens' London, filled with boutiques and restaurants and boasting a Dickens-on-the-Strand festival each December. It is here in a little magic shop that "The

Gentle Art of Reappearing" unfolds, borrowed from the plot of *The Tempest*.

The late 1950s and early 1960s produced some of the most memorable teen rock music prior to The Beatles. It was all about love and both happy and tragic endings. Men and women were idealized as angels—angel babies, earth angels, angel eyes—and some actually found themselves on the other side. What if a boy found himself in heaven by mistake and had to be escorted home by a teen angel with a crush on him, and then the plot reversal required the boy to actually be in heaven to escort the angel back to earth for one more day? The wheels turned and *A Midsummer Night's Dream* became "Bob Weaver and the Teen Angel," with the sentimental music of the 60s.

The truth must be known. These plays are not serious imitations of our beloved Shakespeare's works, just little exercises in extending the wonderful ideas about love and laughter and happy endings that he lent to our own lives. The plays are intended for students to read, to act out in class, or to produce for their parents and classmates, but above all, to help us all remember the depth of passion and humor in our interactions and the one who most eloquently illustrated them, William Shakespeare.

Circle Dance

DANCING AROUND THE MADNESS OF
TWELFTH NIGHT

"Circle Dance" is a short two-act play that mirrors the zany plot of Shakespeare's comedy *Twelfth Night*. Although some of the characters and events have been altered to accommodate a modern high school teen culture, their basic traits remain intact, as do their actions, a testament to the universality of Shakespeare's plays. Events that were not suitable to replicate are now represented symbolically or metaphorically. For example, in *Twelfth Night*, Viola and Sebastian are twins who are separated after being shipwrecked, each believing the other has perished. Modern audiences might find it difficult to accept the same fate, as well as the disguise that confuses Sebastian for Viola, in a play about teenagers. Therefore, in "Circle Dance," Joe drenches his sister-like best friend Lucy with a barrage of water balloons, and Lucy reciprocates with a vase of water thrown in his face. In a sense, they "drown" their relationship and the battle between long-time friends results in a subsequent separation and temporary demise of friendship.

As for the disguise, Lucy does not pretend to be a boy, as Viola does in Orsino's court, to gain the attention of Dave Orson. She uses her wits to become the mystery contributor to the school newspaper for which Dave is editor-in-chief. She is wise beyond her years, and her philosophizing in her "Battle of the Sexes" articles soon attracts the attention of the teenagers in need of advice at Thomas Knightly High School. They are bewildered but intrigued by their own naïve attempts at love, a slow dance that seems to spin out of control as the play moves toward its finale.

Each character in "Circle Dance" retains something of his or her counterpart in Shakespeare's version. Maria Hernandez loves revenge, a good scheme, and Toby Milch. Toby is obsessed with food, especially snacks wrapped in plastic, but he too loves revenge, especially on Malcomb Hightower, the antithesis of Toby. The name Hightower should give the reader a clue about his connection to Shakespeare's Malvolio. Malcomb, comfortably operating in his superego, sets himself above the average student with his love of academics and his sense of righteousness, both taken to an extreme. Andy Andrews, III is Sir Andrew Aguecheek. A follower who is easily manipulated, Andy wants what the others want, to be loved, but the only way he knows how to get it is to submit to Toby's extortion: a portion of his weekly allowance in exchange for the promise of a date with Olivia, which never quite materializes. The character Olivia closely resembles Shakespeare's beautiful young Olivia who seems to have it all, including a string of hopeful suitors who want to share in her good fortune. Although Frank Greene, a member of the newspaper staff, does not have the breadth of character that Feste does in *Twelfth Night*, his one catalytic act of unveiling Lucy's disguise as the mystery writer elevates him to a Feste-like level. His role is absolutely essential in moving the plot to its resolution.

The title that suggests the image of dancing in a circle is both symbolic and metaphoric. Dancing in a circle implies magic— conjuring and creating and protecting what is enclosed. Love, after all, is the theme and worth protecting, whatever the cost. The dancers, moving to the rhythm of the universe, create the archetypal circle of life, death, and rebirth. What follows all our attempts at love is the hope for a rebirth of the spirit. One either holds on to the pain of loving and languishes in it or is transformed by the redemptive, healing power of the experience. Yet the metaphor of dancing in a circle can also express movement that goes nowhere, perhaps taking one back to the place of beginning rather than advancing ahead. The madness of the dance in all its chaos spins like a top. It is the "whirligig of time [that] brings in its revenges," as Feste concludes in *Twelfth Night* (5.1.399-400).

In the end, the play is not meant to be a reflection of the darkness of Shakespeare's play. "Circle Dance" offers instead an expose on both the strengths and weaknesses of the human spirit as well as the tension that ironically does not repel but serves as a magnet to draw people together in love and friendship.

Circle Dance

A PLAY IN TWO ACTS

Synopsis of Scenes

The action of the play takes place in three locations, the bedroom of Lucy Viola, the newspaper office of Thomas Knightly High School in Houston, Texas, and the high school commons.

Act I

Scene 1: Late afternoon, the day before school starts in August in Lucy's bedroom

Scene 2: Afternoon, opening day of high school, in Lucy's bedroom

Scene 3: Next day in the school's newspaper office

Scene 4: Later that day in the commons

Scene 5: A week later in the newspaper office

Scene 6: Friday afternoon in the newspaper office

Act II
Scene 1: Monday morning in the commons
Scene 2: Next afternoon
Scene 3: Saturday night
Scene 4: Monday morning after the dance in the newspaper office

Characters:

Lucy Viola: freshman girl at Thomas Knightly High School

Joe Sabatini: freshman boy and Lucy's best friend and next-door neighbor

Maria Hernandez: Lucy's friend and Toby Milch's new girlfriend

Dave Orson: senior at Knightly and editor-in-chief of the school newspaper *The Knightly News*

Frank Greene: senior at Knightly and newspaper staff reporter with a humor column

James and Michael: freshman JV football players and Joe's buddies

Olivia Carmichael: freshman at Knightly and Lucy's friend

Toby Milch: senior at Knightly and Olivia Carmichael's cousin

Andy Andrews, III: freshman at Knightly who follows Toby Milch around

Malcolm Hightower: senior valedictory hopeful at Knightly

Robert, Will, Ben, Alicia, and Sandra: newspaper staff reporters

Veronica Perez: dance instructor at Dance Studio One

ACT I

SCENE 1

Lucy is lying on her bed talking on the phone. Her bedroom does not appear to be the typical frilly bedroom of a pretty high school girl. No pinks, no ruffles, no lace—it looks more like a dorm room with posters of Betty Friedan, Edna O'Brien, Sylvia Plath, and Albert Einstein. A computer is situated on her desk while books and magazines are scattered and stacked in every other available space. A vase of fresh flowers seems somehow out of place. One might be tempted to call it clutter, but clothes and shoes and other accessories are neatly put away. With the exception of a mug sitting near the computer, no dishes with half-eaten meals lie about. The room gives the impression of a scholarly haven. It's late afternoon, the day before the first day of the new fall semester at Thomas Knightly High School.

Lucy: Why do you say guys can't be friends with girls? I can be friends with a guy. I don't have a problem with that. (*She listens.*) But . . . . but . . . (*She listens.*) Okay, okay, so there might be a little tension, but nothing two people can't deal with. Not everyone is attracted that way, you know. I read this article in *Seventeen* the other day about guys and girls being attracted to the way they smell. Can you imagine going around sniffing people to see if you like them or not? (*She giggles.*) Hey, where are you? I'm hearing an echo. (*Joe opens her door; he's on his cell phone.*) A-a-a-ah! (*She falls off the bed in surprise.*)

Joe: Wha-a-a-t?

Lucy: Don't you knock?

Joe: Knock? (*The term seems foreign to him.*) It's just me. We're like . . . you're like my sister.

Lucy: And you *have* a sister. Do you barge in on her, too? I mean, I could be naked? (*He leaves, closes the door, and knocks.*) Go away. (*He comes in and just stands there. She turns her head to look at him.*) Oh, are you still here? I told you to leave. You're really getting on my last nerve, Joe.

Joe: A-a-w-w. (*He pretends to be hurt.*) Okay. No more talk about girls trying to be friends with guys.

Lucy: (*She sits up and faces him.*) Okay, you can stay. (*She asserts her argument one more time.*) But try to see my point. Guys need to see girls as . . . Oh, I don't know, maybe in the same way they see other guys. I mean, like people, not the opposite sex but like another human being, just someone they can talk to.

Joe: Too complicated. Guys don't wanna talk. They just want things easy. Give 'em something they can fix quickly, without any hassles, so they can be normal again.

Lucy: Normal? You gave up *normal* years ago.

Joe: (*He frowns.*) Play fair.

Lucy: Look, the real problem with guys is that they don't understand what a girl needs. If they would just talk more, they would know. She doesn't want you to fix anything. She just wants you to listen.

Joe: Talk more? How can I talk more if I'm supposed to be listening? (*He smiles now, as if this is entertaining.*) Besides, I am listening.

Lucy: Not now, dummy. I mean when she has a problem, when she needs someone to listen. You know, a shoulder to cry on.

Joe: Oh, no. No, no. (*He picks up a stool, blocking Lucy as if taming a lion.*) Not crying. I can take anything but that.

Lucy: Don't be a wimp. What if she's counting on you? Are you going to just walk away and leave her sobbing . . . alone? As usual, we're going in circles again. Getting nowhere. It's like they say, can't live with them, can't live without them.

Joe: *Them* could also be girls, you know. I could say the same thing, you know. Anyway, you think too much . . . just let things happen. Can I borrow your nail clippers? (*He looks at his nails.*) My mom won't let me eat with the rest of the family till I cut 'em. (*He takes on a sarcastic tone.*) She's threatening to put my dinner on the floor next to Winkie's bowl.

Lucy: Let's see. (*He holds up his hands.*) Gross. At least cats are supposed to have claws. Yours look more like Freddy Kruger's. (*She picks up the clippers off her dresser.*) Here. (*She holds on to the clippers.*) I want them back. (*He starts to leave but turns around.*)

Joe: I like 'em this way. I can scratch better.

Lucy: Go home.

Joe: Look, Lucy, you don't understand guys any more than we understand you. Don't say I said this, but guys are Neanderthals. They like things simple. You Jane, me Tarzan. They see the opposite sex as fish in a large pond waiting to be caught with the right bait. (*He starts to frame a picture with his hands.*) Look, this is how I see it. (*He speaks playfully now.*) Here she comes swimming by in bright blue with little silvery things all over and one of those soft wavy tails . . . .

Lucy: Enough, Fish Man.

Joe: Or maybe a cute little catfish with whiskers.

Lucy: We had catfish for dinner last night.

Joe: What? You don't like my little fish story? You're the one who
           likes all that literary stuff. Besides, my little fish story is . . .
           symbolic. You like symbolism. In fact, everything's really
           symbolic, even sports—oh, yeah, *sports symbolism.* I like
           that. (*He uses his macho football voice but also tries to make
           her laugh, which isn't working.*) Conquest. Victory.

Lucy: Okay. This is too much. This discussion is over. Goodnight,
           Joe.

Joe: Oh, yeah, and here's something else you need to think
           about. I have a news flash for you. Say the word *friendship*
           and you've just given a guy the kiss of death.

Lucy: *We're* friends . . . and no one's dead yet. (*She mutters. She's
           tired of this discussion.*) Yet.

Joe: (*He hesitates.*) That's different. You and I, we . . . . (*He
           smiles.*) We played together in your wading pool half-naked
           when we were three, we gave each other chicken pox when
           we were six, we got our first zits together right before the
           eighth-grade dance. We're only three days apart. We could
           have been exchanged at birth. You look a little like my sister,
           you know.

Lucy: Enough, Joe. (*She sighs.*) You're hopeless and I'm tired. Go
           home. I need to get my sleep. Tomorrow is the first day of
           school and I'm not going to show up with circles under my
           eyes.

Joe: Oh, come on, it's not hopeless. Just accept it. Guys and girls
           can't be friends because neither of 'em wants to be!

The phone rings. She picks it up.

Lucy: Hi, Olivia. What's up? (*She turns to Joe.*) See you later. (*She
           speaks back into the receiver.*) Hey, did you get the dress?

Joe: Who's that? (*Joe grabs a magazine and sits in a comfy chair near the bed.*)

Lucy: Really? What's it like?

Joe: What's *what* like?

Lucy: (*She looks in Joe's direction, perplexed.*) I'm sorry, what'd you say? Who's going out with Frank Greene? You're not serious. Why would she do that? The guy's Looney Toons!

Joe: Maybe she just likes cartoon-y kinda guys. Why do you always have to get involved? Anyway, who's Frank Greene?

Lucy: (*She turns to Joe.*) Will you stop! (*Joe shrugs, flops on the floor and begins reading one of Lucy's magazines.*) No, no, sorry, Olivia. I was just trying to stop Joe from interrupting me. No, you don't know him. He's only my next-door neighbor who came to borrow nail clippers and IS NOW LEAVING. (*Joe frowns but gets up to go. He pats Lucy's head on his way out.*) No, you do NOT want to meet him. He's not your type. Besides, he's got some weird, chauvinistic ideas about guys not being able to be friends with girls. (*She listens.*) Him? Please. I assure you there's nothing going on in that department. (*She listens again.*) Well, that's different. He's my neighbor . . . . He's like my brother.

Curtain

SCENE 2

Lucy opens the door slowly and trudges in looking forlorn. Her hair is stringy and wet, plastered to her head and face. She looks as if she has been caught in a rainstorm, but the sun is shining. She sits down in front of a dressing table and looks in the mirror, picking up a strand or two, then giving up. She plops down on her bed and stares above her. There is a knock on the door.

Lucy: If you've come to apologize, forget it. You're dead meat, Sabatini! History, you hear?

Maria: (*She peeks her head in the room slowly.*) It's me. Maria. Your mom said you were up here. (*She looks at Lucy's hair.*) Whoa! What happened to your hair! Did you just get out of the shower?

Lucy: Yes. I stick my head in the shower whenever I'm mad. You should try it.

Maria: Really? (*Lucy glares up at her.*) Oh . . . well, what are you so mad about? (*She plops down on the bed.*) First day back must have been a disaster. What happened? Didn't you get the classes you wanted?

Lucy: I'm gonna kill him. I'm gonna write in bright red marker on every stall in every girls' bathroom at school: "For   a good time, call Joe Sabatini . . . 852-7441."

Maria: (*She gets up and walks over to Betty Friedan and sits on the stool a short distance from Lucy.*) Lucy, I haven't seen you this mad since Toby Milch demolished your birthday cake an hour before your party. You wanted to smash his face into the rest of the cake but you just kept screaming at him. I'll never forget that day. You can really scream loud. Poor guy. He just stood there in shock.

Lucy: (*She sits up.*) What is it with these guys? You want to like them. You need to like them. They're even likeable most of the time. You can't eliminate them from your life—you need them. But then they go and do something so incredibly stupid and you wonder if they aren't aliens come to destroy the world, or worse, stay and take over.

Maria: (*She speaks sheepishly.*) So what did Toby do this time?

Lucy: (*She sighs.*) It wasn't Toby this time. It was Joe.

Maria: Joe Sabatini ate your birthday cake?

Lucy: Maria, remember? (*She picks up a strand of wet hair.*) My hair? My *wet* hair?

Maria: (*Maria looks puzzled.*) Oh. Joe Sabatini did something to your hair? I thought you said . . . .

Lucy: Okay, sit down. (*Maria sits on the edge of the bed.*) Whole story: Joe Sabatini and his new jock friends were leaning over the second floor railing with water balloons after school today. I got ambushed, Maria. By four water-filled latex bombs. Three really. I think this poor, unsuspecting kid behind me got the other one.

Maria: (*She starts to laugh uncontrollably. Lucy gives her a look.*) Sorry. It's just so . . . . The thought of it is so funny. I love water balloons. Last summer my cousins were here from Beaumont and we sneaked up behind these really buff lifeguards at the pool and we really let 'em have it. Were they mad! We ran so fast Jason almost lost his trunks. They tried to keep us out of the pool for two weeks, but we snuck back in. (*She is whining.*) It was really hot last summer. So, you didn't take a shower?

Lucy: (*She mutters to herself.*) Is everyone insane? (*She looks at Maria, trying to make her understand.*) I feel totally betrayed.

Joe Sabatini may be stupid sometimes, but he's also my oldest friend. We go back a long way, and I can't believe he would do this to me. He humiliated me. How can I ever face all those people again. Everyone was laughing at me. I had to leave school like this. Riding the bus is bad enough, but with everyone staring and asking the same question over and over?

Maria: (*She tries not to laugh.*) Well, there's only one thing to do. Get back at him and make it really good. (*She is getting excited.*) Want some help?

Lucy: (*She falls back on her pillow.*) As much as I'd like that right now, I just can't do it. Besides, I'm through with him. He's as good as gone. I'm not even going to waste my time. (*She grumbles.*) Even though he still has my nail clippers . . . and my Spanish dictionary . . . and my tennis racquet. The guy's a leech. I wonder how he's going to manage without me.

Maria: So, how was your first day? (*She looks away, not waiting for an answer.*) Mine was so-o-o good. (*She giggles.*) I was almost late to my first-period class. I think I'm in love.

Lucy: (*She sits up, feigning a spark of interest in her voice.*) Oh, yeah? Who's the lucky guy? Do I know him?

Maria: Hmmm, actually, you do. I've known him for years, too. I used to think he was such a dork, and he always had his hand in a bag of chips, but, Lucy, he's so-o-o cute now. Over the summer he put something in his hair, I think. Anyway, he's so-o-o cool now.

Lucy: Well, who is this Romeo?

Maria: Um, it's . . . well . . . it's Toby. Toby Milch.

Lucy: (*She pauses, looking at Maria, trying to fathom what she has just heard.*) You're kidding, right?

Maria: No, but, Lucy, wait till you see him. He's so-o-o cute.

Lucy: Whatever makes you smile, Maria . . . . (*She turns and rolls her eyes. There is a knock at the door. Lucy looks but doesn't move.*) Don't answer it. (*The knocking continues. Maria starts toward the door. Lucy puts her hand up to stop her.*)

Joe: (*He speaks from the other side of the door.*) Lucy? I know you're in there. Your mom said you were. Open up, ple-e-ase? I need to talk to you. I'm sorry. Really. I'm really, really sorry. (*There is no sound.*) Lucy, don't do this. You're my best friend.

Lucy: (*She jumps up, picks up the vase, throws the flowers on the bed, and opens the door.*) If you think this is how best friends treat each other, great. Now, it's my turn. (*She throws the water from the vase in his face as Maria gasps.*)

Maria: Cool.

Curtain

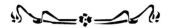

SCENE 3

Lucy opens the door to the office of the school newspaper, The Knightly News. *The room looks like a typical classroom-turned-newspaper-office, with tables, computers, soda cans, pizza boxes, old newspapers, empty coffee mugs, and other clutter. She is clearly here for the first time, as she looks around a bit unsure of herself. Two boys rush around busily from their computers to tables of papers. Another boy is sitting at a table reading copy. Dave, the editor-in-chief, sits at a computer, staring straight ahead. No one notices her come in.*

Lucy: Excuse me. (*She waits. There is no reply. She speaks again, louder.*) Excuse me. Is this where you apply to work on the newspaper staff?

Dave: (*He stops his gaze to turn his head in her direction. He looks her over before speaking.*) Did you register for journalism?

Lucy: No, I'm afraid it wasn't offered at a time when I . . . .

Dave: (*He swivels his chair to face her.*) You're a freshman, aren't you?

Lucy: Yeah, how did you know?

Dave: (*He gets up and walks toward her with his hands in his pockets, taking advantage of his senior status.*) Freshmen can't sign up for journalism or the newspaper. You should know that. Can you write?

Lucy: I *like* to write.

Dave: Well, Miss I-Like-to-Write Freshman, I hope you can write better than some of these Bozos around here. We've got three good writers on this paltry staff and about fifteen mediocre ones, *when* they show up on time, and I could occasionally use a sub. Can you cover a story? Do you know what to look for? Do you have the guts to run with a lead and stand by it?

Lucy: Well, I don't know, but I'm not afraid to speak what's on my mind.

Dave: What's your name, little fishy?

Lucy: Little fishy? (*She laughs, amused at his attempted put-down.*) It's Lucy. Lucy Viola.

Dave: Look, Lady Violet . . . .

Lucy: Viola.

Dave: Don't confuse having a mouth on you and having the guts to dig out facts for a story.

Lucy: (*She is getting defensive now but preparing to play the game.*) I'm not sure about mouths and guts, but I do have brains and fingers and I can even make them work together.

Dave: (*He smiles at being challenged.*) Well, well. If you can make your brains *and* fingers work as well as your mouth and guts, I might be able to use you. What have you written?

Lucy: (*Opening her notebook, she gets out a sheet of paper with writing on it.*) I brought a sample.

Dave: (*He scans the pages quickly.*) Not bad, not too bad. (*He tosses pages at her.*) You can fill in as backup. Can you stay after school? Do you have transportation? Can you cover something at the last minute?

Lucy: Yes, no, yes.

Dave: Listen, you're an okay writer and I can probably throw something your way, but right now we don't need anybody else. (*He starts back to his chair. Lucy follows him.*)

Lucy: I can pick up. You know, stack things, keep things in order, make coffee.

Dave: Rule number one: DON'T . . . TOUCH . . . ANYTHING! All right, listen. Here. (*He hands her a dollar bill.*) Get me a Coke, no sissy Diet Coke, either. Just regular Coke, got it? (*She nods, takes the money, and starts to leave. A boy comes through the door waving a British flag. It's Frank Greene who writes a humor column for the Knightly News.*)

Frank: (*He waves his flag in Lucy's face.*) Hello, mates.

Dave: What's with the Union Jack, buddy?

Frank: (*He feigns an English accent.*) I pinched it off the Queen of Hearts, ol' chum.

Dave: A-a-w-w, sweet. Hey, Frank, meet Lucy, fresh off the boat, our latest fish. She's gonna fill in when some of these goof-balls around here can't get their articles done, so you better be on your toes or you just might find her writing YOUR column.

Frank: (*Back to his old self, he glares at Lucy.*) No way.

Dave: She's going for cokes now. Anybody want one? (*Two reporters wave him off.*)

Frank: (*He slips back into the accent.*) A spot of Sprite, please. (*He reaches into his pocket for change, hands it to Lucy, who leaves to get drinks.*)

Dave: (*He grabs the flag.*) Frank, shut up and put the flag down. Anyway, where'd you get it?

Frank: Seriously, this hot new freshman girl was handing out flags to the best-looking senior men on campus. I got this one. You know how freshmen girls can't resist us senior men.

Dave: So you've paid a visit to the Model UN booth in the commons, huh, Frank? (*He chuckles.*)

Frank: No kidding, man. The girl at the booth was so hot. I haven't seen that much talent the three years I've been here. I couldn't take my eyes off her face. And then she smiled at me, man. I thought I was gonna . . . .

Dave: Yeah? What's her name? (*He is getting interested.*)

Frank: You think I don't know, but I'm not stupid. I looked at her nametag. OLIVIA . . . .

Dave: I thought you couldn't take your eyes off her face. Olivia what?

Frank: Olivia Who Cares? What does it matter to you anyway? I saw her first.

Dave: I need a date for the fall newspaper dance. Something nice attached to my arm would be just right.

Frank: Oh, no you don't, you traitor. She's mine. I saw her first.

Lucy: (*She walks back into the room with two sodas.*) Saw who first?

Dave: Our man Frank here is a prime example of good investigative reporting, Lucy. He's sniffed out a story. Seems like there's a . . . something exciting at the Model UN booth down in the commons that needs checking out. I think we should go downstairs and investigate the . . . . uh . . . capital of Bolivia. (*They start to rush toward the door.*)

Lucy: Oh, you mean Olivia.

Dave: (*He stops suddenly.*) You know her?

Lucy: Olivia Carmichael. We went to the same school last year. She's a good friend of mine. She's running the Model UN booth downstairs and then she's coming over to my house later.

Dave: (*He shuts the door.*) Lucy, Lucy, Lucy. I knew you were going to be good for this paper. What do you know about this girl? Give it to me in one minute or less.

Lucy: Five-two. Green eyes. Long brown hair. Good grades . . . .

Dave: Okay, that's enough. Let's go. Frank, gimme that flag.

Dave leaves, followed by Frank and two reporters.

Lucy: (*Looking around, she realizes she is alone.*) I can't believe it. I'm a reasonably smart person. Will I ever understand guys? Are the laws of attraction not based on any logic at all? When a guy is interested in a girl, what makes him lose rational behavior? Where's the rule book that explains how to get it back? Why doesn't somebody teach us this stuff before it's too late? (*She sits at a table, opens her journal, and begins writing. She picks up the book and reads aloud.*) "The Peace Process: The Impossible Dream?"

Curtain

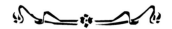

SCENE 4

Joe and several members of the junior varsity football team walk toward a table in the commons in the center of the school. At a table up left is Toby Milch, his new girlfriend Maria Hernandez, and a new freshman, Andy Andrews, who seems to be following Toby around. At a third table Malcomb Hightower, a well-known candidate for valedictorian of the senior class, sits with his head in a book, apparently studying. Every now and then, however, he looks at his calculator and then glances quickly in the direction of the Model UN booth. Olivia Carmichael is standing behind a table, and close observation reveals that he is more interested in Olivia than the calculus on which he appears to be working. The sign behind her reads, "Join Model UN today! Find your international voice here." Flags of different nations adorn the table.

Joe: (*He walks in with a coke in his hand laughing, apparently at a joke from James and Michael, two of Joe's new football friends accompanying him.*) That's a good one, man. Hey, I bet you haven't heard this one. Okay, see there's this guy and he stops at this farmhouse after he's been walking for about three days and . . . . (*He stops when he sees Olivia at the booth. James and Michael sit down at a table up center.*)

James: So he's been walking for three days and then?

Joe: (*He leans over to talk to Michael.*) Who's the goddess?

Michael: I dunno. Let's ask her. (*He gets up and swaggers over to her table.*)

Olivia: Hi. Would you like to sign up for Model UN? It'll be lots of fun. You get to represent the nation you choose. Here, you can look over this information and . . . .

Michael: So . . . your name is Olivia. Well, Olivia, I'm here to sign up for Bolivia. (*He laughs and looks at his buddies, who join in the laughter.*)

Olivia: Bolivia? You're making fun of me? Look, if you're not interested in joining Model UN, fine. But don't come over here and waste my time.

James: Ooo, she's so cute when she's mad!

Joe: (*He walks closer to the table.*) Hey, look, he was just playing around. He didn't mean any harm. (*Olivia gives him a look that says, "Oh, really."*) C'mon, guys. Give her a break. Hey, Olivia. I'm Joe. Help us out here. We're just dumb guys who don't know anything about Model UN, and I guess (*He looks at James and Michael.*) less about how to approach a girl. What's it all about?

Olivia: Approaching a girl, or Model UN?

Joe: (*He laughs.*) Touché. Let's start with Model UN.

Olivia: Well . . . . (*Hesitant, she takes a pamphlet and slowly unfolds it without taking her eyes off Joe.*) Our organization is just a smaller version of the UN. Global issues are addressed and . . . . (*She begins to show him the information. He pays close attention. Michael and James are bored. They walk over to the snack bar. In the meantime, at a table down left, another conversation is taking place.*)

Toby: Sure, I know her. That's my cousin Olivia. Why?

Andy: I think I'm in love. She's so beautiful she makes me want to cry.

Toby: No girl will ever make me cry. Onions make me cry. Not having money for food makes me cry. (*He opens a bag of chips without looking.*) Oh, look, onion rings. (*He takes a bite.*)

Andy: What I wouldn't give to go out with that girl. Every guy would go insane when they saw me walking into the dance with her.

Toby: Oh, yeah? Well, for a small fee, I might be able to arrange something. Like a reciprocal agreement, know what I mean?

Andy: A what?

Toby: Didn't they teach you anything in eighth grade? It's like you scratch my back and I'll scratch yours. (*He waits for the light to come on in Andy's eyes.*) I can help you out, man, for a little cash-ola.

Andy: Oh, man, you gotta be kidding. (*He's now very interested in this proposition.*) What! I'll do it, whatever it is. Name your price. Are you serious?

Toby: I don't know. I am running a little low on the green stuff these days. A guy's gotta eat, ya know. How much allowance do you get every week?

Andy: Uh, well . . . . (*He thinks about it a moment.*) I've been getting $50 a week, but I have to buy my lunch, so that really only leaves me about $25 for . . . .

Toby: That's good. First payment will begin . . . now.

Andy: (*Andy digs in his pocket for the money.*) All I have is a ten.

Toby: (*He reachs for the bill.*) That'll do.

Meanwhile Malcolm has been listening to the conversation. His interest in Olivia is more than casual.

Malcolm: (*He walks up to table where Toby is sitting. He speaks to Toby.*) I heard what you said. In a civilized society of ethical people, a transaction such as this one constitutes a crime.

(*Trying to be righteous, he comes across as sarcastic.*) I believe this illegal behavior is called extortion. But the real crime, gentlemen, is the damage done to this girl. (*He looks over at Olivia, still busy with Joe.*) One has only to observe the situation to recognize how this spotless, blameless model of perfection has been tainted by the evil mind of one who would stoop so low as to trade her favor for . . . money. You disgust me! You'd be wise to drop this transaction, or others will know about this, if you understand my meaning. (*Malcolm walks back to his table, his head held high, picks up his books and calculator, and exits the commons, leaving Toby, Maria, and Andy speechless. When Malcolm is gone, the three burst out laughing.*)

Maria: WHO DOES HE THINK HE IS?

Toby: Somebody just elected him president.

Andy: President? Of what?

Maria: Well, he could be president . . . of the math club. (*They laugh.*)

Toby: No way. Without his calculator, he can't even add and subtract. He sure can't count. If he could, he'd know how outnumbered he is. Out-numbered, get it! (*He laughs.*)

Andy: Huh?

Toby: It's a joke, man. (*Toby rips open another bag of chips.*)

Andy: Oh.

Maria: Listen, I've personally had enough of his attitude. He sees himself as better than everybody else. It's getting so bad that you wonder if he snoops around trying to catch people making mistakes or committing crimes just so he can set everyone straight and make himself look good. Like he's captain of the Nice Squad. He needs somebody to put him down in a big way—so much that he'll never bother anyone again.

Toby: Yeah. Yeah, that's right. So what? What do you suggest, my little Cheeto? *(He puts the Cheeto to her lips and then stuffs it in his mouth.)* Lay it on us.

Andy: Yeah . . . lay it on us. *(Toby gives Andy a puzzled look.)*

Maria: It's pretty clear he's hung up on Olivia, right? What if he was made to believe she liked him, too?

Toby: Oh, sure. How's that gonna happen? Girls like Olivia don't give guys like Malcolm the time of day.

Maria: What if he *thinks* she likes him?

Toby: He'd be dreaming.

Maria: Exactly. We create the dream. Here's my plan. We write a letter to Malcolm making him think it's from Olivia.

Toby: Remember this guy is gonna be valedictorian. He's not stupid. He'll know it's not her handwriting.

Maria: No problem. She's your cousin. Can't you get close enough to get a sample of her handwriting? It won't take me long to copy her style. Leave it to me.

Toby: All right! I'm beginning to get the picture and I like it. So what are you going to say in this letter? Tell us, tell us!

Maria: Well, you know the newspaper dance is next Saturday, right? Chances are he doesn't have a date. We'll make him think Olivia wants him to take her.

Toby: Is that it?

Andy: Yeah. Is that it? (*Toby claps his hand over Andy's mouth. Andy slouches back into his chair.*)

Maria: No, wait for it. Here's the best part. In the letter Olivia will say she's wearing a bright yellow dress, and wouldn't it be perfect if he wore a matching suit. Oh, yes, and her favorite flower is the sunflower. And he should probably wear one, too. In his lapel. The guy worships her so much he'll do anything she says without question. At the end of the letter, we'll say she has to be at the dance early, but he can meet her by the punch bowl at nine o'clock.

Toby: Brilliant, my honey bun! (*He takes a bite of the pastry he's just unwrapped.*) Start writing!

Andy tries without success to open a bag of chips of his own. Dave and Frank come rushing in, spot Olivia, and Dave freezes. All he can do is mutter, "**Oh-h, y-e-a-h!**"

Curtain

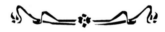

SCENE 5

It's the next day in the newsroom. Dave gathers his staff around him for an announcement.

Dave: Okay, everyone. Listen up. Bigsby, get over here. All right. You guys have really been slow on the ticket sales for the dance. We don't have a rich benefactor, you know. We need to meet our goal to keep this paper running. Ads aren't bringing in enough to cover the costs, (*There are groans from the staff.*) which brings me to the news of the day. We're going to announce to the student body on Friday a dance contest. Since the theme of this year's dance is *Fiesta!* it's going to be a Latin dance contest. (*There are more groans.*)

Robert: Hey, boss, I can't dance. No way I'm getting out on that floor.

Dave: To supplement the income from ticket sales, there will be a small entry fee. I'm making it mandatory that all staff members enter. We've got to show 'em a good example.

Will: No, man. You really don't wanna see me get out there and make an idiot of myself.

Ben: You're already an idiot, William. (*Will swats at Ben, missing.*)

Dave: I've thought about that. Which is why, starting tomorrow afternoon, you'll show up here for complimentary lessons. You've got three free hours of instruction to learn how to make your feet move. Hips, too, from what I can gather.

Alicia: Dave, you gotta be kidding.

Sandra: That's great! My boyfriend and I go out dancing at this salsa club every Friday night. Sign me up.

Will: But I have a date Friday.

Dave: Cancel.

Will: Right. She's not gonna like this. Can I bring her with me?

Dave: Okay. Just SHOW UP. Lucy, you're not officially on the staff, but I expect you to be here, too.

Lucy: Sure. Cha, cha, cha.

Dave: Oh, yeah, one more thing. Someone put an envelope in Mr. Morris's box yesterday with my name on it. (*He holds up the envelope and pulls out sheets of paper.*) Folks, I think we've got ourselves a little mystery writer, and it's pretty good. I'm thinking about printing it, even though we don't have a by-line.

Sandra: What's so good about it?

Alicia: Yeah. What makes this one so great? I have a few pieces we haven't run yet. Use one of mine for a change.

Dave: Stop writing about Paris Hilton's latest boyfriend and I might.

Sandra: Let me get this straight. You're going to print an article written by someone you know nothing about?

Dave: Yeah, I know, but it's a fresh look at an old topic, the battle of the sexes. Nobody ever loses interest in that, and with the dance coming up, it's the kind of thing people want to read about. I really want to run it. I know it's ultimately my decision, but does anyone have any fierce objection to printing it?

Will: Don't you think that's taking too much of a risk? I mean, what if it's a set-up? What if Morris himself wrote it?

Dave: Morris wouldn't do that. He's too ethical and he wants the paper to succeed. And, okay, maybe there are some risks, but it's a better piece than I've gotten from any of you in quite a while. Frankly, we're losing our readers and we're barely covering our expenses. We need something to light a fire under 'em again. I'm doing it. Lucy, I'm assigning you to proofread it. Edit if necessary. (*He hands the piece to Lucy, whose mouth drops open.*) I want it tomorrow morning at 7:30 so I can run it in the next issue. All right, you guys, get outta here and get those articles finished. I want them in the morning before school . . . in this box. See you tomorrow.

Oh, yeah, and remember our dance lesson tomorrow after school.

(Everyone leaves. Lucy pulls out her notebook, looks around, gets sheets of paper out, slips them into the box on Dave's desk, and quickly exits.)

Curtain

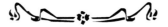

Scene 6

In the newsroom Dave and the staff have pushed tables and chairs back to make space for a dance floor. He's brought in a dance instructor for the afternoon, and salsa music is playing. The staff sits around the room nervously watching and waiting. A few stragglers enter and join the others.

Dave: Okay, you guys. Gather 'round. This is Veronica Perez from Dance Studio One, and she's agreed to spend three hours teaching you some basic steps. (*He looks at Veronica.*) Ready?

Veronica: Hi, everyone. Call me Ronnie, okay? It's nice to be here. We're gonna grab a partner and make a big circle around me. You're gonna learn the basic steps for the salsa, that Latin beat of love! First, just watch what I do and then we'll try it together. Okay, hold your partner like this. (*She demonstrates with Dave who doesn't have a partner. Everyone watches. Lucy looks around for a partner. They're all taken. She decides to dance by herself.*) Okay, kids. Now let's salsa! Ready? Watch my feet. Off we go! (*Ronnie notices Lucy doesn't have a partner and drags Dave over to her, putting them together to practice.*) That's it. Now remember your footwork and your hip motion. You got hips, now wiggle them!

(The partners practice. Most are struggling to remember the steps but some are just trying to make their feet work. One couple seems a bit stiff, no hip action. Another couple has a little too much movement. Lucy and Dave seem to be experiencing a little success. Ronnie shows Dave how to turn Lucy so that his arms are around her as they face the front. Everyone on stage freezes. Dave closes his eyes and smells her hair. They have stopped. Lucy turns slowly to face him and they stare into each other's eyes for a moment before they break apart. Lucy rushes over to the chair to retrieve her purse.)

Lucy: I have to go now. Sorry . . . *(She looks at her watch.)* . . . have to go. *(She runs out the door.)*

Curtain

ACT II

SCENE 1

  The second act opens in the commons. It is Monday, the week of the dance. Students who have congregated begin talking about the event. At a table up center are Toby, Maria, and Andy. At another table down right are Olivia and Lucy, and at a third table down left are Dave, Frank, Will, Robert, and Sandra. The next issue of the paper is out and people are reading. In fact, all you can see are newspapers covering everyone's face. The hot topic is, of course, the mystery writer. Dave is gloating over the success.

Toby: Hey, Orson, 'bout time you gave us something worth reading.

Andy: Yeah . . . *(He pauses before going on, looks at Toby, and shrinks back.)*

Maria: Who's the new mystery writer, Dave? *(Dave smiles but says nothing.)* Come on, you can tell us.

Dave: You know I can't reveal my sources. (*Lucy starts to leave; Olivia pulls her back into her seat. She is clearly interested in the conversation.*)

Olivia: It has to be a girl.

Dave: (*He turns to look at her.*) What makes you so sure of that?

Olivia: Trust me. Guys don't know that much about relationships. Besides, the writer uses details. Guys don't do that. They generalize.

Dave: (*He gets up and walks two steps to the table next to him.*) I have to disagree with you. (*Lucy looks at Dave but says nothing.*) Think about all the journalists who write every day. What percentage are men? Do you think only women can observe and write about details? More men than women have won the Pulitzer.

Olivia: And what percentage has written about relationships? (*Dave pauses, unable to respond quickly. He's mesmerized by her as she gets up and faces him.*) Face it. Women have the advantage of default behavior, thousands of years of tribal clanship, the millennia of women discussing relationships over cook fires after a long day of gathering nuts and berries.

Dave: (*Looking out to the audience, he is perplexed and confused.*) What?

Toby: (*He has put* The Knightly News *down to listen. He speaks to the audience.*) That's it? Thousands of years gathering nuts and berries makes women experts on relationships? Yeah, I guess that says it all. Feed us and we're yours.

Maria: Here, have another honey bun . . . honey bun! (*Toby obliges her by taking a bite.*)

Dave: (*He gets up again and crosses to Olivia.*) Hey, look, uh . . . Olivia, right? (*She nods.*) Why don't we continue discussing this over a frappuccino down the street?

Olivia: Sorry. I promised Lucy I'd study with her at the library this afternoon. (*Lucy puts her paper down, smiles, and nods her head.*)

Dave: (*He glances at Lucy, frowning.*) Okay, well how about the dance Saturday night?

Olivia: Sorry again. I've got a date.

Dave: Oh. Who with?

Olivia: Joe Sabatini. He's a freshman football player. JV quarterback.

Dave: Well, good for you. If you change your mind, give me a call. (*He walks back to his table and talks to Frank.*)

Lucy: (*She looks at Olivia, astonished.*) Joe Sabatini plays football now? You know him? (*The agitation in her voice grows.*) You're actually going to the dance with that deceiving water-balloon bombing traitor?

Olivia: Calm down! It's just a date. Aren't you being a little hard on him? What did he ever do to you?

Lucy: Olivia, don't you remember the first day of school when Joe and his jock friends ambushed me on the landing with water balloons? Remember on the phone when my neighbor Joe came over to borrow nail clippers and I said you didn't want to meet him. Being a bit hard on him? Oh, as far as I'm concerned Joe Sabatini doesn't exist. He's a non-entity.

Olivia: And why exactly didn't I want to meet him?

Lucy: He's not your type.

Olivia: Lucy, I'm crazy about him. He is SO my type. He's so cute and so sweet. I can't believe we're talking about the same guy.

Lucy: I thought I knew him. (*Her tone is softening now.*) The thing is . . . the thing is, he was my best friend. I mean, there could never be any romantic involvement, but we literally grew up together. Our parents have been best friends since we were babies. We've always lived next door to each other and well, we've been like brother and sister. He taught me how to ride a bike when no one else would help me. (*The anger is returning to her voice.*) But what he did to me—I'm not sure I can forgive him . . . .

Olivia: Oh, Lucy. I wish you could be friends again. He really seems like such a nice guy. He just made a stupid mistake. Guys *do* that, you know. Besides, I know a secret. (*She leans in toward Lucy and glances around her for eavesdroppers.*) You know that mystery writer Dave Orson was talking about? The one who wrote that great article we all loved on the battle of the sexes and making peace and everything . . . . (*She looks at Lucy as if she has just had a revelation.*) Hey, maybe you should read it again. It might help you with Joe.

Lucy: Yeah, what about it? (*She frowns.*)

Olivia: I know who it is.

Lucy: (*She is getting uncomfortable.*) You do?

Olivia: Yes. It's Joe Sabatini. (*She unfolds her newspaper and finds the article.*) Look at this. (*She shows Lucy a paragraph.*) That theory about people being attracted to each other's smell—I never heard that until Joe told me about it—on the telephone last weekend. That was before the paper came out, Lucy. I know it's him. It has to be.

Lucy: You've been talking to him on the phone?

Olivia: Lucy, have you been listening to anything I've said?

Lucy: Okay, but didn't you just tell Dave that you thought the mystery writer was a girl?

Olivia: I was just trying to throw him off. Joe's the one guy who really understands what a girl needs. (*She takes her mirror and lipstick out and begins to apply it.*)

Lucy: (*She puts her head in her hands.*) Oh-h-h-h-h.

Olivia: Oh, my gosh! It's four o'clock. We gotta get out of here if we're going to study. I have to be home by seven. (*They quickly gather up their backpacks and exit. Lucy's notebook slips out and remains on the floor by her chair. The snack bar manager wipes the table, picks the journal up off the floor and lays it on the table. With some interest, Frank walks over to the table, picks it up and looks at it, then looks at the door, and opens it. He begins reading.*)

Frank: (*He is still reading.*) Well, whadya know!

Curtain

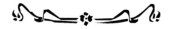

SCENE 2

The scene opens on the next afternoon in the commons. Toby, Maria, and Andy are sitting at a table.

Andy: Look, I can't stay here any longer. You said you could get me a date with Olivia, but she won't even look at me. She gives all her attention to that Joe guy and none to me.

Toby: Be patient, my man. She's just being a woman. You know how they like to play hard to get. It's all in the chase. I heard her tell Lucy that she wished they could be *friends* again. If you ask me, she's waiting to meet her prince. Eh, Prince Andrew, heh, heh, heh.

Andy: Do you really think so?

Toby: Would I lie to you?

Andy: (*He looks at Toby like he is finally catching on, but hope prevails.*) Okay, but I can't wait forever. The dance is only a few days away.

Toby: That's the spirit! (*He slaps Andy on the back*) Hey, listen, my good friend, I'm a little short of cash and the feedbag's empty. Can you spare me, say, a five? (*Andy reluctantly digs in his pocket and produces the bill.*) Thanks, pal. I'm working for you. (*He gets up to go to the snack bar to spend his new cash.*)

It's lunch time. Dave and Lucy enter and walk toward the snack bar to buy sandwiches and chips.

Dave: Olivia will listen to you. Please talk to her for me. Tell her how great I am. Lie if you have to. (*Lucy laughs. They sit down at a table down right.*) Look, we've become good friends. I'm really glad you walked into the newspaper office that day. You're one of the best writers we have and you're only a freshman. (*She gives him a warning look that says he's going too far.*) Okay, so you're old for your age. But my point is we get along and you know me. Talk to Olivia and tell her she should go out with me.

Lucy: (*She is getting serious now.*) But what if she just can't? I mean, say there's a girl who has the same feelings for you that you have for Olivia. What would you say to her? That no matter how you feel, you'll put your true feelings aside and go out with her anyway? Just because she likes you? It doesn't work that way, Dave. It *shouldn't* work that way. Relationships—and that includes friendships—should be based on mutual respect and trust. And being a perceptive listener! (*Dave looks as if he is searching his memory for something. He begins looking through the newspaper for the answer.*)

Dave: Where have I heard that before? Didn't I just read that somewhere?

Lucy: (*Quickly guiding him to another point, she takes the paper away from him and folds it up, realizing she must divert his attention from the clue she has carelessly tossed him.*) Well, if you've just read it, why didn't you listen to it? The fact is the media has been trying to pound this into guys' heads for the last decade, at least. Don't you watch *Friends*?

Dave: (*He sighs.*) Okay. I guess you're right. Maybe I'm not supposed to take anyone to the dance. Like fate, huh.

Lucy: Oh, come on. (*She puts her hand on his shoulder in mock comfort.*) It's not that bad. I'm going by myself, too. If you're lucky, I'll ask you to dance. You know, salsa, that Latin beat of love! (*Mocking the dance instructor, they begin to dance around the room laughing.*)

Curtain

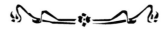

SCENE 3

The dance is under way in the commons. Balloons, streamers, colorful paper flowers, and piñatas adorn the room. Rock music plays as couples dance. When the music stops, Dave finishes his dance with Lucy and walks with her to the punch bowl.

Dave: Thanks, Luce. You're really a good dancer. (*He pours her a cup of punch.*) You can write, you're really smart, you're cute—for a freshman (*He playfully pats her head.*) and you can dance. So why don't you have a boyfriend?

Lucy: Who says I don't?

Dave: Oh. Well, where is he? You've never mentioned having a boyfriend. I just assumed . . . .

Lucy: Things are seldom what they seem.

Dave: So, what's he like?

Lucy: About your age.

Dave: No good. You need to date a freshman. That's the mistake all freshmen girls make. They're flattered when senior men want to date them, but when they take the bait and go out with seniors, who eventually graduate, it takes a long time for these girls to get back into the dating pool. Be smart, Lucy. Date a guy your own age so you can spend your senior year together and not end up like me, without a girlfriend to do things with. I mean, like tonight for example. Look at all these couples who've been together. They can count on someone to be there for them.

Lucy: What have you been doing all this time? Chasing illusions?

Dave: You know something, sometimes you act like you're really old. You're starting to sound like my mother, and it's scary.

Lucy: I read a lot. (*She changes the subject.*) Look, Dave, you're the editor-in-chief of the school newspaper. That's no small thing. You got early acceptance into Yale while other people were playing the social scene. You were doing what you had to do to get to the top.

Dave: Well, you know what they say. It's lonely up there. (*There is an uncomfortable silence as they look at each other.*)

The door opens and Malcolm Hightower walks in. He is wearing a yellow suit and has a bouquet of large sunflowers in his hand. There is a smaller sunflower in his lapel. He walks over to the punch bowl looking at his watch. He then spies Olivia and rushes over to her. Gradually all of the students look in his direction and laugh. It appears the only one he sees is Olivia.)

Malcolm: Hello, Olivia. Here I am. You look beautiful. (*He hands her the flowers, which she takes reluctantly.*) But I thought you were going to have on a yellow dress. (*He looks at his own bright yellow outfit.*) To match my suit. (*Olivia is speechless. He looks at Joe and it dawns on him that she is with him. He leans in to speak to her.*) I've come here to be with you. Why are you with him?

Olivia: Malcolm, thank you for the flowers. That was so sweet, but I don't know what you mean. What are you talking about— yellow dress? (*He pulls the letter from his coat pocket and hands it to her.*) I'm here with Joe. Joe is my date. (*She reads the letter. When she looks up, she sees Toby doubled over in laughter.*) Oh, no. Malcolm, I'm so sorry. (*She walks toward Toby, holding the letter up.*) I get it. You did this, didn't you. You wrote this. Why?

Toby: (*He backs up like a coward.*) Hey, I didn't write it. Maria did. (*Maria hits him on the arm. He winces.*)

Olivia: Out of my sight, you brute. (*Although the music continues, many of the couples have stopped dancing.*) Do you think of no one and no *thing* but yourself and food? Why do you think you can take advantage of people and hurt them like this? I'm really disappointed in you, Toby. After that embarrassing cake incident at Lucy's, you promised you would stop. Sometimes I'm sorry to be related to you.

Toby: It's no big deal. You're overreacting. We were just having a little fun.

Olivia: I'm sorry, Malcolm. (*Toby has stopped laughing. He and Maria exit with Andy following behind them. Toby finally pushes Andy away. Andy moves over to a table and sits by himself.*) I'm sorry, Malcolm. (*He is looking sad and bewildered.*) I didn't write this. I would never have done this to you.

Malcolm: (*He takes the flower from his lapel and throws it on the ground. He starts to leave but turns around for one last word.*) Oh, don't you worry. I'll have my revenge on the whole lot of you. (*He exits.*)

The dance has temporarily halted as the spectacle with Malcolm ends. Dave goes to the mike to make an announcement.

Dave: Okay, everyone, the judges are ready with their decision. (*He opens the envelope and looks at the card.*) The winning couple in the first annual Newspaper Ball Latin dance competition is . . . . Olivia Carmichael and Joe Sabatini. Congratulations! Come on up and receive your trophies. (*Olivia and Joe excitedly step forward. Dave hands them their prize and the crowd applauds.*) And now, if music be the food of love, play on . . . . (*The music resumes, a slow dance this time, and Olivia and Joe begin the dance. Frank rushes up to the mike.*)

Frank: Hold on, everyone. We've got another surprise announcement. (*The music stops and there is a buzz from the crowd.*) Several weeks ago, the newspaper staff received the first of its feature articles on the battle of the sexes. It caused quite a stir and for a while everyone wanted to know who the mystery writer was. Well, my friends, tonight I'm going to let you in on the secret. *The Knightly News* mystery writer with the olive branch is . . . drum roll, please (*Lucy moves toward the door.*) our very own little freshman . . . Lucy Viola! (*Everyone gasps, surprised at the information, but they applaud as if another award has been bestowed. Olivia and Joe both exclaim to each other,* "**Lucy?**" *Lucy has already made her escape.*)

Olivia: I'm going after her. (*She looks at Joe and heads for the door.*)

Joe: Wait, I'm coming with you! (*They exit together.*)

Curtain

SCENE 4

The curtain opens on the newsroom. It is late afternoon. Dave is sitting at his computer, but his feet are up on the desk, his hands behind his head. He seems far away. Lucy opens the door slowly. She enters and walks quietly over to a table to retrieve the journal Frank has left for her.

Dave: (*He quickly looks up to see Lucy has come in and turns back around.*) You could have told me.

Lucy: (*She stops at the table and answers. She can't look at him.*) Could I really? You mean you would have published the controversial articles of a freshman girl you didn't know? (*She turns and walks toward Dave.*) Wasn't it because there was an air of mystery that you used them and kept on printing them? Wasn't that the real reason? I wanted to tell you, but then things got out of hand and I . . . I just couldn't. I was afraid you wouldn't like me any more. I thought you'd throw me out of the newspaper and I . . . .

Dave: Lucy . . . .

Lucy: Don't. It's okay. I'm quitting. I won't be back. I just came to pick up my journal.

Dave: (*He gets up and moves toward her.*) No, Lucy. Don't go. You don't have to quit. I don't want you to leave . . . . I mean, you're one of our best writers. You *are* the best writer. You're looking at editor someday.

Lucy: I'm so embarrassed. Why did Frank have to announce it at the dance? Why did he have to say anything at all? I felt so . . . foolish.

Dave: Foolish? You ended up having a hugely popular column that woke everybody up. No, not foolish. More like . . . brave. As for Frank, I don't know. You know Frank. He likes getting attention. He knew something no one else did and for a moment he had a little power. I have to say, I was pretty surprised. I actually thought the mystery contributor was Joe Sabatini, that guy Olivia was with Saturday.

Lucy: (*She is surprised.*) Why? Why him?

Dave: I guess because he was new on the scene and he was with Olivia. When she insisted it was a girl writing the column, I thought she was trying to cover up for Joe.

Lucy: Well, that Joe guy is my next-door neighbor. I've known him all my life. He's like my brother. He can't even write his own essays without my help. The weird thing is, Olivia thought it was Joe, too, so maybe she did think she was protecting him. In a way I understand. Joe and I have argued endlessly about relationships. It's scary, but now that I think about it, we probably do say the same things, maybe even use the same words. Sometimes even the same philosophy. All that time, I thought we disagreed about everything. We've been really good friends for so long; maybe we're too close. You know how people in families feel so safe with each other that they argue all the time? Anyway, thanks to Olivia, we're friends again.

Dave: Friends again?

Lucy: (*She laughs.*) It's a long story.

Dave: So why aren't *you* with Joe?

Lucy: He's like my brother. The thought of kissing Joe would be, well . . . like kissing the back of my hand.

Dave: Here, let me see. (*He takes her hand and studies it with mock seriousness. Then, to the surprise of both of them, he kisses it.*) Hmmm. Not bad.

Lucy: (*Feeling suddenly shy, she laughs awkwardly.*) Right. Well, I have to go now.

Dave: What about the paper?

Lucy: I don't know.

Dave: You could continue the column—"The Battles of the Sexes: Peace in the War Zone." (*He grabs the Union Jack and starts waving it.*) What do you say?

Lucy: It wouldn't be the same with a by-line.

Dave: Things change.

Lucy: I'm not so sure. What's that saying? "*—plus c'est meme chose, plus ca change.*"

Dave: The more things change, the more they stay the same, right?

Lucy: Something like that.

Dave: Lucy, you might not have put your name on it, but you were honest about a lot of what you said. This whole attempt at relationships is such a game. Nobody fully understands the rules, but an unknown came in—a freshman girl, and gave a little insight to some kids in desperate need of advice. At least you gave them something to think about. You can't stop now.

Lucy: Can I think about it?

Dave: Sure. The paper goes out on Friday. (*She nods and walks to the door but hesitates as if she doesn't really want to go.*) Hey, listen, the staff's meeting at Tony's this afternoon to celebrate "fiscal success." (*He grabs his backpack to go.*) We're in the black again. Wanna come? (*She pauses and looks at him. He holds out his hand. She looks at him briefly and then takes it. They head for the door.*) Now, about that line from Betty Friedan. You might want to rethink using those feminist tactics of yours . . . (*Lucy groans. They exit and the battle continues . . . .*)

Curtain

Bob Weaver and the Teen Angel

A 1960S MUSICAL IN TWO ACTS

In *Midsummer Night's Dream*, Shakespeare introduces a number of couples who must work out their differences before tying the knot. Hermia wishes to marry Lysander, a respectable young Greek, but her father insists that she wed Demetrius instead. Since love must triumph in Shakespeare's romances, and the penalty for disobeying one's father is death or a nunnery, the couple has little choice but to make a run for it. Demetrius is not to be outdone and he goes after them into the woods where the two have escaped, only to be followed by Hermia's best friend Helena, who incidentally is still in love with her old flame Demetrius.

Magic is added to the mix with King Oberon and Queen Titania of the Fairies and Puck, Oberon's sidekick who does his master's bidding with the juice of a flower. An important subplot is the story of Bottom the Weaver whose merry friends decide to audition for the Duke's wedding day entertainment. They will present a play, a re-enactment of Pyramus and Thisbe, but Bottom is in the wrong place at the wrong time. Oberon and Puck turn him into a man with the head of a donkey, whom Titania, whose eyelids have been touched with the magic juice, will fall in love with the first creature she sees upon waking, as punishment for not handing over the boy to Oberon. Shakespeare gives us a lighthearted scene with mixed up choices to laugh at ourselves as well as his foolish characters because we all have made silly mistakes. In the forest, the symbolic life of refuge and safety, Shakespeare transforms the characters' fears and weaknesses and struggle for power into a haven of love where everything hoped for is, in the end, realized.

Take the essential theme of Shakespeare's play, with some modern twists, and Bob Weaver finds himself, not in a forest, but in a mistaken situation where he, too, must find a way out and back to reality. The subplot in this little play is reversed. It is Bob's story against the backdrop of the lovers who must find a way to be with the right partner.

Synopsis of Scenes:
Act I
Scene 1: The Regis family home
Scene 2: A wooded park across the highway from the high school
Scene 3: A waiting room, entry level of Heaven

Act II
Scene 1: The wooded park
Scene 2: Deeper into the wooded park
Scene 3: The junior/senior prom

Characters:
Regis: Irma's father
Damian: High school senior and golf partner to Regis, who has chosen Damian for his daughter
Irma: Regis's daughter, a high school senior who is in love with Lester
Lester: Irma's boyfriend
Bob Weaver: A senior, Pyramus in the skit, who finds himself in Heaven by mistake
Jimmy: A senior and the Wall in the skit

Barbara: A senior and Thisbe in the skit

Angela: An angel in heaven and receptionist for The Chief

Mr. Speldt: A elderly man, hard of hearing, waiting to get into Heaven

Mrs. Harker: An elderly woman, missing her dog and waiting to get into Heaven

Mrs. Applegate: An elderly woman who loved gardening, waiting to get into Heaven

The Chief: No explanation needed

Prof. Harold Winegold: An elderly man, also waiting to get into Heaven

Joe: A senior and the Lion in the skit

Student announcer for the skit

Sid: A senior and Moonlight in the skit

Patti: Barb's sister, in charge of music for the skit

Miss Blossom: Senior English teacher

Phil and Alison: Seniors at the prom

Liz: A senior girl at the prom

ACT 1

SCENE 1

It is early April 1963. Regis, a middle aged man who has clearly been successful in life, arrives home after a morning of golf. He has an eighteen year old boy in tow, obviously a golf companion according to his attire. They are pleased with themselves, teeming with manly enthusiasm as they enter boasting about their game. The young man, Damian, is not just a golf partner. He is the father's pick as a partner for his only motherless daughter.

Regis: One of our better days on the course, eh, Damian?

Damian: Right you are, sir. Your swing is unbeatable, Mr. Regis. I'd like to be as good as you one day.

Regis: It's all in the wrist, son. But keep working on it. You'll get there one day. Say, how about a nice cold soda? Root beer do? Put hair on your chest. (*He laughs and slaps his chest.*)

Damian: Sure, Mr. Regis. That'd be great. (*Regis leans down to a small refrigerator located behind the bar and returns with a bottle of root beer.*)

Regis: Now, where is that daughter of mine? You know, son, I was hoping you'd be the one standing at this door the night of the prom.

Damian: It would be an honor for me to escort Irma to the dance, sir, but do you really think she'd go with me?

Regis: Damian, my boy, I'm not only king of the course . . . You just leave the details to me. You see, it's a lot like business. You have to pull the right strings and the moment you know you've got 'em, you quickly wrap up the deal. Women aren't any different.

Irma: (*She walks in with her boyfriend Lester.*) Women aren't any different from what, Daddy? Oh, hi, Damian. Did you and Dad enjoy your game of golf? (*Not waiting for a reply*) Oh, Daddy, Lester and I are going to a movie and then we'll probably just grab a burger at Judy's. I won't be late, but don't wait up. (*She leans in to kiss his cheek.*)

Regis: Hold on there, little girl. You aren't going anywhere. I have reservations at the club tonight and I've asked Damian to join us. In fact, you need to go upstairs and get changed now. We'll wait.

Irma: No offense, Damian, but (*looking at Regis*), I have a boyfriend, in case you've overlooked that fact. His name is Lester, the very boy standing in this living room, and we've been dating forever, at least six months. I keep trying to tell you. Daddy, when are you going to start noticing life outside a golf course?

Regis: All right. That's quite enough, little miss. Young man, I think you'd better leave now. My daughter and I have a few things to discuss.

Damian: Sir, I think I need to be going, too.

Regis: No, sir-ee bobtail monkey, you stay right where you are.

Irma: Lester's not going anywhere, either. Daddy, you're embarrassing everyone with this ridiculous behavior. I'm going up to change. Lester and I have a study date tonight.

Lester: Irma, that's okay. I'll go. Pick you up Saturday at seven?

Regis: I wouldn't bother, son. She's not going. I've had enough of this disrespect.

Irma: Disrespect? Daddy! Why are you doing this? I can't believe you would keep me from going to the one dance every senior waits for . . . . for four years! How could you do this to me? (*Lester shrugs, shakes his head and walks toward the door. Irma looks at Damian who doesn't budge.*) You'd better go, too. I need to talk to my dad alone.

Regis: Son, just wait outside the door. (*Damian steps outside.*)

Irma: If only Mom could see you now. She wouldn't believe it, and she certainly wouldn't let you carry on like this.

Regis: Leave your mother out of this. I've got plans for you, and if you don't have the good sense to listen to me, I'll have to make decisions for you without your help.

Irma: Without my help? This is crazy, Daddy. I've made terrific grades, good enough to get into State. You know I've always wanted to be a nurse. Aren't you proud of that? Once upon a time you didn't seem to mind that I made that decision.

Regis: Irma, Irma. The truth is all that talk of college isn't going to get you anywhere. You need to start thinking about finding a husband who can take care of you. Someone like Damian.

Irma: Oh, I see it all so clearly now. You've chosen a *husband* for me? That's convenient for you. What about what I want? Lester is my boyfriend, Dad. I choose Lester.

Regis: Then you choose not to go to the prom. Furthermore, I'm sending you to stay with your Aunt Gracie in Maine . . . . on the farm . . . . twenty-two miles from town.

Irma: Okay, Dad. Stop. I'm not going anywhere. That's clear across the country in the middle of nowhere. Would you really separate me from all my friends and the last summer we'll spend together before everyone leaves for college? That's . . . . cruel. How could you do that to your only daughter? Besides, who'd cook dinner every night? (*Irma turns away, and she and Lester head for the door.*)

Regis: Where do you think you're going?

Irma: I'd like to say goodnight to Lester. (*She and Lester leave without waiting for a reply.*)

Regis: (*He opens the front door where Damian is still waiting.*) Damian, come on in, son.

Damian: Are you sure, sir. Things don't sound too good. (*Regis looks sharply at him.*) But, I guess you're the boss!

Regis: That's right. Everything's going to be fine. Just fine. (*Damian squeezes in past Irma and Lester.*) Now, if you still need a date to the prom, Irma's your girl. She'd be glad to have you escort her, that is if that's all right with you.

Damian: Sir, I'm not sure your daughter feels the same way. She was pretty upset.

Regis: Son, one thing you're going to have to learn. You see, women don't know what they want, or even what's good for them. Now, I don't want to push you into anything you don't want to do, but . . . . (*He pauses*) trust me. I know my daughter. She'll come around. (*Damian walks to the door.*) But, son, there's just one thing I need you to do.

Damian: Sure, Mr. Regis. What can I do for you, sir?

Regis: (*He begins singing "Take Good Care of My Baby."*)

Damian: Well, sir, that *is* thinking ahead, but if you say so, sir. (*He turns back to Regis.*) Oh, and thanks for the game, Mr. Regis.

Regis: The pleasure's all mine, son. All mine.(*He takes a long drink of his root beer. Before Damian can leave, there is a knock at the door. Regis answers it. It's Helen. She looks surprised to see Damian.*)

Helen: Oh, hello, Mr. Regis. Is Irma home? I was hoping she could help me with my chemistry homework. (*Damian comes closer and Helen can't stop staring at him.*)

Regis: Didn't you just see her? She's saying goodbye to Lester . . . . (*He looks out*) right outside this door. Hmm. Looks like they're gone. What's going on?

Helen: Hello, Damian.

Damian: Helen.

Helen: How've you been? Going to the prom this weekend?

Damian: Well, I, I'm not sure.

Helen: I guess we're not still on for that, are we. (*It isn't really a question so she doesn't wait for an answer. Clearly whatever was between them has changed.*) Well, if things don't work out and you still need a date, I'm still available. We could go as . . . . friends?

Damian: Uh, well, I—

Regis: (*He has returned from outside the door.*) Young lady, I'm sorry. Damian here is escorting my Irma to the prom. But, hey, plenty of those young folks will go by themselves. That's what we did in my day. Had a real good time, too.

Helen: Thanks, Mr. Regis. You'll tell Irma to call me?

Regis: Sure thing, Helen. Night, now. (*He closes the door.*) They're gone. She's left with Lester! Where in the world . . . .

Damian: I think I know, sir. If you'll excuse me, I'm on my way over there now. (*He exits.*)

Curtain

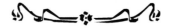

Scene 2

The scene opens in a wooded park across the highway from the high school. Irma and Lester enter from upstage left.

Irma: Ugh. These shoes are killing me. Why didn't you tell me we'd be walking to your aunt's house a hundred miles away?

Lester: Sit down here. It's not a hundred miles. It was just to the highway and here we are. Look, there's the road and there's the school. Rest your feet for a few minutes and then we'll hitch a ride. It's only 26 miles from here.

Irma: (*She sits on the bench next to Lester and takes off her shoes. He begins massaging her feet.*) You take such good care of me. What would I do without you? You're an angel. My angel baby. (*She begins singing "Angel Baby."*)

Lester: Well, your father might have an answer to that. He thinks you'd be much better off without me. In fact, he seems to have your whole life planned, including Damian. I don't stand a chance. Anyway, what's he got that I don't?

Irma: (*She hesitates and then smiles.*) Um, he plays golf?

Lester: Golf. Great. That's just peachy. I lose your father's approval because I don't play golf.

Irma: Lighten up, silly boy. I'm just kidding. You worry too much. Damian likes Daddy more than he likes me.

Lester: What?

Irma:	Money, Lester. Damian's interests lie in what Daddy's money can do for him—his gas stations, the diner, his real estate business. I'm just his ticket to the good life.
Lester:	Oh.
Irma:	Besides, honey bun, after we're married, you won't have a thing to worry about.
Lester:	Married? We haven't even graduated from high school yet. I don't even have a job, Irma. How'm I supposed to take care of you?
Irma:	You can go to work for my dad, and I can go to nursing school. Easy.
Lester:	I don't know about that little plan. Got anything else?
Irma:	Anything else? I thought you loved me.
Lester:	I'm eighteen, Irma. I'm a high school senior with no prospects. What are we going to live on when your dad *doesn't* give me a job because he's just employed Damian, golf wonder boy? I've been thinking about college, too, you know.
Irma:	College? But that's four years!
Lester:	That's right. The same four years you'll be in nursing school.
Irma:	What about all our plans? Everything we talked about? Dreamed about? All gone up in smoke?
Lester:	We'll still have each other no matter what. What's four years?
Irma:	An eternity!

Lester: Now you're being impossible.

Irma: Fine . . . . that's it. I'm going home. (*She starts to get up and put her shoes back on.*) We're finished if that's how you feel.

Lester: Irma, wait! (*Music begins and the shrubbery comes alive and begins singing the introduction to "Breaking up Is Hard to Do." Lester sings the song, with the "shrubbery" singing backup vocals. When he finishes, there is a moment of awkward silence and then he moves closer to her.*) Wanna piece of gum? It's Juicy Fruit. Your favorite.

Irma: (*She smiles, forgetting her frustration, and takes the gum.*) Oh, all right. You're just too cute, you know that.

Lester: Aw, shucks. You're pretty cute yourself . . . . Nurse Irma. Wanna take my temperature? I'm feeling awfully warm. (*They rub noses.*)

Irma: Well, college man of my dreams, we'd better get going. What time did you tell your aunt that we'd be there? Quick! Someone's coming. (*Suddenly a noise from behind makes both exit quickly off right. Bob Weaver, another senior, and two of his classmates, a girl and another boy, enter from upstage and cross to the benches. They have chosen this spot to rehearse a skit that will be part of the entertainment for the senior prom.*)

Bob: Stop here. This looks like a good spot. Get your scripts out, guys. Jimmy, we'll start with you.

Jimmy: (*He reads from his script.*) "Oh, wall, oh hateful wall . . ." (*He begins singing with his air guitar.*) "Don't keep me away from my ba . . . by—"

Bob: No, no, no. No singing yet.

Jimmy: But it's good. It's like, I should be singin' to Thisbe, the woman I love.

Bob: Stick to the script, Jimmy.

Jimmy: Okay, okay. Whatever you say. You're the boss. (*He begins again.*) "But for you, wall, we could touch and kiss and—

Barbara: Hey, watch where you're putting those hands, buddy.

Bob: Jimmy, what are you doin'? We've only got a few days 'til the prom. Keep it cool, man. Do it again.

Jimmy: If we had a real wall, it would be easier. How am I supposed to touch the wall and kiss it when there's just air between us? Besides, Barb keeps moving. Make her be still. So's I don't get distracted.

Barbara: I didn't move! You did!

Bob: Enough you two! Start from your line, Barbara.

Barbara: (*She gives Jimmy a warning look.*) "At least you give a passage for loving words to reach loving ears, and for that we are so grateful."

Jimmy: (*He's singing again.*) "Oh, the night has a thousand eyes, but baby, I need your lovin'." (*He stops singing as Bob begins to protest.*) "Meet me at the tree near the fairgrounds tomorrow and we'll steal away, together, just you and me, (*singing again*) together, forever."

Bob: Okay, cut. Let's do the scene with the lion now. (*He looks around for Joe.*) Where's Joe?

Barbara: He had after school detention.

Bob: Well, did you tell him to meet us here after he got out?

Barbara: I don't remember. I think so.

Bob: (*Exasperated*) Okay. You two go through the scene again and I'll go look for him. Keep him here if he gets here before I get back. And try to get it right this time. (*He exits up left.*)

Barbara: So, Jimmy. Who're you taking to the prom Saturday?

Jimmy: I dunno. Didn't ask anyone yet.

Barbara: Yet? It's a little late for that. No girl with any self respect would even consider going at this late date. (*The screeching, squealing sound of an automobile slamming on its breaks can be heard. Barbara, gasping, looks at Jimmy in fear and they exit quickly up left.*)

Curtain

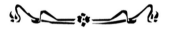

Scene 3

The scene opens in a large room with only a row of seven chairs facing the audience with various people sitting in them. At the end of the row, stage left, sitting behind a desk is a pretty teenager dressed in white and wearing sparkly white cat-eye glasses. Bob enters from the right and takes the empty seat on the end.

Angela: (*She looks over her list and checks it with a long white feather pen.*) Mary Bruner? (*The woman in the first chair gets up and walks to the desk. Everyone moves up a chair.*) I'm so sorry, Mrs. Bruner, but you need to complete the back of your application as well. (*She assists her.*)

Bob: (*He leans in to talk to a white haired man sitting next to him.*) Hi, there. Say, are we waiting for something? Is this the doctor's office? Or maybe the dentist? Can't be the principal's office. I've been there enough times, and I know what that looks like. What's this piece of paper for?

Mr. Speldt: What's that, son? Speak a little louder.

Bob: I said, (*increasing his volume*) where am I? What's the name of this place?

Mr. Speldt: Fish face? Who's a fish face? Did you just say *fish face?*

Bob: No, sir. I asked you if you knew the name of this place.

Mr. Speldt: What?

Bob: Here, give me a pencil.

Mr. Speldt: No, I'm not ill.

Bob: (*He motions writing on the man's application.*)

Mr. Speldt: Yes, yes. You'd better write it down. Hearing's not what it used to be. (*Bob writes his question.*) Oh, is that what you were saying. I could have told you if you'd just spoken louder. (*He pauses.*)

Bob: So where are we?

Mr. Speldt: Not rightly sure, son. I don't remember applying for a job. Haven't worked in years. Maybe it's heaven. I just remember sitting in my chair—the real comfy one—and I was listening to gospel music on the radio when I just drifted off. Last thing I remember, Mahalia was hitting a high note.

Mrs. Harker: (*Sitting to the left of Mr. Speldt*) Oh, it's heaven, all right. Must be. I never go anywhere without my little Noodles. She was sleeping in my arms when it happened, and if she could, she'd be right here with me.

Bob: When *what* happened?

Mrs. Harker: My little dog Noodles and I were sitting in front of the television watching the Lawrence Welk show when a car came right through the picture window in the front room. Right through the picture window! All of a sudden it was dark and a minute later I was sitting in this chair. Oh, I do hope I can see my precious little Noodle poodle again soon.

Angela: Next! Professor Harold Winegold? Everyone, please move to the next seat. (*All move over and leave a seat empty at the end of the row. A woman in a gardening apron and hat enters and takes the chair. She still has gardening tools in her apron.*)

Mrs. Applegate: (*She slowly looks all around her with a confused expression on her face, taking a garden tool from the pocket of her apron and gazing at it.*) I must have forgotten to take my apron off. Is this Dr. Phillips' office? I'd been meaning to make an appointment all week. (*Angela gets up and hands her an application on a clipboard and a pen, then returns to her desk.*) I wonder how I got here. I don't remember driving. (*She looks at the application, taking a pair of reading glasses from another pocket. She reads from the application aloud.*) "Name three animals that survived because of your actions on earth." Well, that one's easy. You know, my husband could just never bring himself to kill those chickens. So we just kept on feeding them till they died of old age. We had a real nice funeral for each and every one. Such a sweet little bunch of hens, especially the one we called Mrs. Chickwick. One Easter I made her a bonnet and painted her nails bright pink. (*She begins singing and swaying to "Easter Parade."*)

Bob: (*He looks at the application and reads the next question aloud.*) "Number 2. Name ten people whom you truly loved." Whoa, Nelly! Ten? I'm not sure I know ten people I really *like*.

Mrs. Applegate: Oh, go on, give it a try. You seem like such a nice young man. You must have loved lots of people. I bet the girls thought you were a real catch.

Bob: Well, (*counting on his fingers*), there's my dad and my mom. And then there's Gran and Grandpa Bob—I was named after him. Let's see, that's four. I guess I can count my younger brother Skip. Most of the time he's okay, I guess.

Angela: Next in line, please. (*She smiles and speaks in a cheerful sing-song way.*) I believe that would be you, Dr. Harris. (*A man in a white doctor coat goes to her desk and waits.*) Everyone, move up, please. (*They all get up and move.*)

Bob: If I can't name ten, what happens?

Mr. Speldt: Maybe they send you to the other place?

Mrs. Harker: No, I think that's just a rumor. I don't believe there is another place. There's just one big office building and all the people and dogs and cats and even chickens get to live as one big happy family.

Mrs. Applegate: Why, I do believe you must be right. Dear, it's your turn.

Mrs. Harker: (*She looks back toward Angela's desk.*) Oh, my. So it is. (*She looks at her three companions.*) Well, goodbye to you all. May we meet again on the other side. (*They wave and say good bye.*)

Angela: Come along, Mrs. Harker. Don't forget your application. (*Mrs. Speldt hands it to Mrs. Harker. There is a silence as they all continue filling in the blanks. Mrs. Harker exits.*) Henry Speldt? Ready? (*He has not heard her and continues to write.*)

Bob: I think she means you, sir. Are you Mr. Henry Speldt?

Mr. Speldt: (*He stares at Bob, then at Angela.*) Yes, yes, I'm ready. Good luck, son. (*He shakes Bob's hand and goes to Angela's desk, handing her his form. They talk briefly and he exits.*)

Bob: (*He gets up and quickly walks to her desk.*) Listen, uh, Miss, I think there must be some mistake. I haven't lived long enough to be here. Didn't you notice I was the youngest person in this line?

Angela: I can assure you, Mr. Weaver, the Chief doesn't make mistakes. (*She continues writing without looking up.*)

Bob: Look, why don't you just use that telephone there to call whoever it is you talk to, and I'll just go sit at the end until you find out I'm right. (*He walks toward the empty seat.*)

The Chief: (*In a deep, loud voice only*) Sit down. Please. (*Bob looks around and hesitates.*) Now. (*Bob returns to his seat and taps his food nervously.*) And be quiet.

Angela: I'm ready for you now, Mr. Weaver. Step forward.

Bob: (*He walks slowly to her desk, looking at her face.*) Why am I here?

Angela: (*She has lost her happy sing-song tone.*) I'll ask the questions, if you don't mind. Have you filled out the appropriate forms? (*She takes his application and looks it over.*) Thank you. Don't worry. This is just the entry level, to welcome newcomers.

Bob: · Newcomers to what? When can I go home? I have a play to produce and a senior prom to attend. People are expecting me to—

Angela: (*She leans forward and speaks in a low tone.*) You really don't get it, do you? You're in heaven now and you should be very happy. (*She looks up again as if something has just occurred to her.*) Prom? Did you say *prom*?

Bob: Sure, you know what that is. That thing where you get all dressed up and dance to some really cool music before you graduate.

Angela: Yes, yes. I know what it is. I—I just haven't heard that word in—what seems like an eternity.

Bob: (*He smiles, getting more comfortable.*) Well, I guess talking to a girl like you, I must be in heaven. I'm usually not so good with girls, as you can see on my application. (*He leans forward to show her the application.*) See there, number two. You know, that love question.

Angela: (*She blushes, softening her tone.*) I assure you, Mr. Weaver, very few people, even the older ones, can think of ten people they really love.

Bob: What's your name?

Angela: Excuse me?

Bob: (*He begins singing "What's Your Name" and the people sitting in the chairs sing backup vocals. Angela shuffles papers around on her desk, finding little tasks to keep her busy so she doesn't have to look at him.*)

Bob: (*He moves closer to her.*) Your name. You have a name, don't you? (*He continues singing.*)

Angela: (*She is taken off guard and seems surprised.*) Stop, really. It's . . . . Angela. We don't usually refer to our names that we had on earth but I still remember . . . . Is it really *prom* time?

Bob: (*He laughs softly.*) Sure is. So, you're an angel named Angela. Cool. (*He boldly takes off her glasses and she doesn't resist him.*) Angela, the angel talking to a teen angel who ends up in heaven—by mistake. Hey, I ought to write a play about that.

Angela: (*She looks at her list.*) Sorry, Bob. Actually, someone else gets to write that one. You'll have to try again.

Bob: Will I have the chance? (*She looks at him for a moment. Both are silent.*) I'll bet you were an angel on earth, too.

Angela: Oh, yes, well . . . . I really don't remember. Sometimes I try to remember. I shouldn't be talking like this. (*She puts her glasses back on and looks at the list again.*) What did you say your name is? Robert Earl Weaver?

Bob: Earl? No way! My parents actually couldn't decide on a middle name, so it's just Robert. Robert Weaver, but everyone calls me Bob.

Angela: Robert Weaver? (*She reads the list aloud.*) Robert Aaron, Robert Earl, Robert Wayne . . . . Oh, my God—(*She looks up.*) Oh, sorry, Sir. I don't see your name anywhere on the list—no one without a middle name. (*She nervously picks up the receiver and dials O.*) Sorry to bother you, Sir, but the young man at my desk doesn't seem to be listed on the current roll. Perhaps, there's a more up to date list . . . . No, no, Sir. I wasn't doubting you. It's just that I've looked up and down the list—(*She turns her back to Bob.*)—but he's just not here. Could it be . . . . a . . . . mistake? No, I know, Sir, You are, well, *You*, after all, and You don't make mistakes. (*She whispers now, turning away from Bob.*) But what should I do? (*She listens, pausing.*) Right, right, yes, right. Of course, thank you, Sir. (*She looks back at Bob.*) Bob, uh, Mr. Weaver, the Chief says you should sit and wait at the end again until it can be decided what's to be done with you. (*Bob reluctantly begins to walk away but returns to the desk.*)

Bob: (*He perches on her desk.*) Why can't I just sit here and talk to you? (*He continues singing—Is it Mary or Sue?.*)

Angela: (*She looks up at him with pleading eyes.*) Really, Mr. Weaver, you must stop singing. Please, sit down. I actually have work to do. (*He walks away dejectedly. She watches him and then calls, "Next!" A woman gets up but stops as the phone rings. Angela quickly answers it.*) Sir? (*She pauses.*) A mistake, Sir? But You . . . . You don't . . . . Yes, Sir. I understand. (*She puts the receiver back and looks at Bob.*) Mr. Weaver, step forward, please. (*He rushes to her desk.*) There has indeed been a . . . . mistake. The wrong boy was promoted.

Bob: *Promoted?*

Angela: Yes, I know. (*She begins to straighten her desk and get her things.*) It's the new terminology around here. The Chief applies euphemisms whenever possible. Says it creates a more positive approach to finalizing. (*She pauses.*) Anyway, I've been assigned to assist in your realignment. (*She walks around to the front of her desk. Another angel, a young man, enters and takes her place. He begins looking at the list. In the meantime, all the seats are full again, as more people have entered.*)

Bob: *Realignment?*

Angela: Getting back is a bit tricky, but obviously not impossible—what with that whole miracle thing and "anything is possible" agenda—especially since you never got past pre-registration.

Bob: Whoa! I don't quite follow you.

Angela: I'm taking you back to earth, Bob.

Bob: (*He begins dancing with her and singing the chorus of "Pretty Little Angel Eyes." He then grabs her, twirls her around, and kisses her. She is startled and can hardly move.*) Oh, sorry. I got carried away.

Angela: (*She recovers and pretends to be annoyed.*) Yes, well, try to behave yourself. If you want to get back in one piece, we have to do this right.

Bob: Do what?

Angela: Follow me. (*She walks downstage and points to a circle drawn on the floor and flooded in light.*) Stand in this circle and count to three. It will reconfigure the molecular structure of the body and send it to the particular destination of your choice.

Bob: Cool! Can anybody use this?

Angela: No, the Chief has the only access to the controls and no one has ever seen either one. There's actually going to be a television program one day that uses this idea but it won't happen for at least three years. The guys who are going to write the script are working on the idea now. Are you ready to go? (*They step into the circle. She holds his hand. He looks at her and smiles.*)

Bob: This is amazing . . . . hitching a ride from heaven to earth holding my angel's hand. (*He begins to sing "Pretty Little Angel Eyes."*)

Angela: (*She shakes her head in dismay or maybe embarrassment.*) We're ready, Sir.

The Chief: May the force be with you.

(*Lights come down as John Williams' theme music from Star Wars comes up.*)

Curtain

ACT II

Scene 1

The scene opens with Angela in the same forest where the three teenagers had been rehearsing their skit, a spinoff of "Pyramus and Thisbe" for the prom. Bob does not seem to be with her.

Angela: Trees! I'd forgotten how beautiful they are. (*She touches the bark lovingly.*) So many colors! The sky, clouds, grass, flowers, leaves. Oh, I have missed all of you. Look how the light shines through the leaves. (*She hears a loud noise and races upstage.*) There's a highway! Cars, trucks whizzing by. It's all so exhilarating. Did I drive one of those? I can't seem to recall, but the memories are coming back to me so clearly. Must remember why I'm here. Bob. (*She looks around.*) Oh, dear. Bob! What have I done with him? (*She hears the three teenagers returning.*) Who's that? (*She hides behind a tree to listen.*)

Joe: Okay, so now we've lost Bob. No telling how long he'll lie in that hospital bed without waking up, poor guy. How are we supposed to finish rehearsing without him? We only have two more days until Prom.

Barbara: You have your script, don't you?

Joe: Sure, but—

Jimmy: It's a good script. We'll do the best we can. To honor Bob, right?

Barbara: Yes, of course. And, Joe, you don't actually have many lines but you do have to growl. You *can* growl, can't you?

Joe: Don't you want me to growl at the right time? And what if the lion comes in during the love scene? Huh? That wouldn't be too good.

Jimmy: Okay, let's not waste any more time. All right, Barb, you enter from the right and look around for Pyramus. Then Lion, you come out and growl. Thisbe drops P's letter jacket and lion mauls it. Ready? Action.

Barbara: (*She enters and looks around.*) Oh, Pyramus, my darling Pyramus. I'm he—re. Baby, where are you? (*Suddenly Joe comes out on all fours, raising up the trunk of his body, his hands pawing the air. He growls and she runs off right, dropping her jacket. Lion pretends to scratch and bite it.*)

Jimmy: Cut! Okay, that works. Joe, you can go easy on the mauling. You don't want to be accused of overkill, would you? Ha! Get it? *Overkill.* (*Joe and Barbara look at him with no expression at all.*) Okay, let's rehearse the end tomorrow after school. It's getting late now. Barbara, when you get home call Bob's house and see what's going on. We need to put the music in the right place. Also you said you would bring the Angels and the Bobby Vee records. That still good?

Barbara: They're right next to my Hi-Fi. I asked my little sister Patti to play them at the right time in the skit and she said okay.

Jimmy: How's she gonna get in to the Senior Prom? She's only a freshman.

Barbara: Don't worry. I've got connections, Angel Baby. Besides, I already asked Mr. Thornhill and he said it would be just peachy as long as she leaves after the skit.

Joe: That little sister of yours—maybe she could be my date. She looks old enough to be a junior. Maybe you could put in a good word . . .

Barbara: Nix on that. You're forgetting—not only does everybody know she's my little sister, but she was also voted most intelligent of the freshman class of 1962. Besides, you're not her type. She's gonna be the first woman on the moon—that's all she can think about—and books, of course. She's a regular bookworm, that girl.

Joe: Why does anybody want go to the moon? It's much nicer just to look at it from down here.

Barbara: Aw, Joe, that's so romantic. I didn't know you had it in you. (*They begin to walk stage left.*)

Joe: (*He exits with Barbara and Jimmy.*) There's a lot you don't know about me. Say, do you want to go to the Prom?

Angela: (*She comes out from behind the tree and sits on the bench.*) There's so much they all don't know. In a few years, three men will get the credit for the first moon landing—not a woman. In fact, poor Patti will never become an astronaut. Oh, well. (*She looks up at the moon.*) It is nice to look at. (*She begins singing a few bars of "Blue Moon."*) Oh, yes. (*She looks up at the moon again.*) You do know exactly what you're doing, don't you. (*She soon hears another noise.*) Oh, dear! Someone's coming! (*She hides behind the tree near the bench.*)

Damian: Why are you following me? Go home. (*He turns to her.*) Look, Helen. It's over between us. I love Irma, now, and her dad likes me, too.

Helen: Irma's dad may like you, indeed, but Irma doesn't. She likes Lester. Don't you understand—Irma has run away with Lester. Eloped, Damian. In case you've forgotten what that means—Besides, you don't really love Irma. I know you too well, remember. We used to be a couple, and not that long ago either.

Damian: (*He stops her.*) You don't know that for sure. Anyway, we're not now. And Irma's too smart to just run away. She wants to go to college.

Helen: Like my mama used to say, I didn't just fall off a turnip truck. Of course, they've eloped. What do you think it means when two people run off together? It may come as a shock to you men, but a girl can be married *and* go to college. (*He walks away, ignoring her question.*) Okay, then go. Go get her. Run after someone you can't have. Ever. (*She begins singing "One Fine Day."*)

Damian: (*He turns around and shakes his head.*) Look, Helen. Whatever we had, it's over. Irma's father is loaded. He owns three gas stations and a diner. I would never be without a job again. And all of that will be mine one day. (*Angela frowns and then jumps up and pulls the white chiffon scarf around her ponytail off.*) Helen, I'm sorry. I like you a lot. It's just that I—(*Helen quickly moves upstage.*) You'll find someone else. You're pretty and nice and smart. But it's not meant to be, Helen. Try to understand that, will you.

Helen: It's not your pity I want, Damian. (*She begins to walk into the forest off left.*) Ugh, why do men have to be so stupid, sometimes?

Damian: (*Angela waves her scarf over his head and he runs after her.*) No, wait! Helen, I didn't mean that. Would you slow down! Helen, wait! Wait!

Curtain

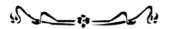

Scene 2

Angela is walking deeper into the forest where she sees Lester and Irma having a picnic of sorts on his jacket spread out on the ground. She observes more closely.

Irma: I'll trade you a bite of my moon pie for a sip of your RC.

Lester: (*Looking forlorn, he hands her the soda.*) Here.

Irma: *Here?* Is something wrong? You've been acting strange ever since we left the park. You're not having second thoughts, are you? (*He doesn't answer.*) Oh, my gosh, you are!

Lester: No, Irma. Nothing's wrong. You worry too much. It's just that, well, what if you decide your dad is right. You know the old saying—blood is thicker than water.

Irma: Oh, great. Look who's worrying too much now.

Lester: You've been so close to your dad ever since your mom . . . . well, you know.

Irma: Died, Lester? Since my mom died? I never even knew her. I was only a year old. And yes, my dad is the only parent I've ever known, but I'm not a child anymore. This is what people do when they grow up. They move on, get married, have—

Lester: All right, all right.

Irma: Although, he was really looking forward to giving me away at the big white wedding. In the church. On the corner.

Lester: See, I told you so. It's that sort of thing that scares me. I don't think I can go through with it.

Irma: What's this all about, Lester? You can't go through with it? You can't marry me? You don't love me? (*Her tone is more and more agitated.*)

Damian: (*He appears from out of the bushes. He is out of breath.*) Have you guys seen Helen?

Irma: Damian, what are you doing here? Helen? Why are you looking for her? (*She walks over to him.*) Still want to go to the prom? (*She turns to see if Lester is watching.*) I just might be available. (*Angela waves her white scarf again over Damian.*)

Damian: Sorry, have to find Helen. (*He exits left, running. Irma sits on the bench with her back to Lester. He sits down next to her for a moment, then puts his hand on her shoulder and turns her around. He begins singing "Devoted to You" and Irma joins in for a duet.*)

Lester: Oh, Irma. I'm so sorry. Can you forgive me for being such a fool? (*Angela sighs and uses her scarf to wipe her brow, in relief.*)

Irma: We've both been foolish. Look, I have an idea. Let's go home and talk to my father, tell him everything, and at least give him a chance to get used to the idea.

Lester: Whatever you say. You're the boss. (*They exit left, arm in arm.*)

Angela: (*She spreads out her scarf and sits on it, looking up at the moon.*) Whew, that was close. I need a rest. Hello, again, you lovely Moon. It's actually quite nice to see you from this side, but really you're not nearly as important where I come from. No offense, but—but here? Oh, boy. The songs that have been written about you! (*She hums and sings "Blue Moon" again.*) Everyone's talking about you. In fact, people can hardly say your name without bursting into song. It sounds like a cliché, but, oh, how I miss it, love I mean. Up there, you don't think about it so much. It's what you might call sterile, one big harmonious happy family *all the time*. You start to lose track of how wonderful love is when you never feel anything but peace and quiet. You begin to long for a moment of conflict just to liven things up a bit. It's enough to put your emotions right to sleep. I was in a play once in high school, right before it happened. "To sleep, perchance to dream." I had dreams once. I don't remember any of them, but I remember having them. I know I'm not supposed to remember things like that, but ever since I landed on earth again, things are starting to come back to me. It's like a word that's sitting on the tip of your tongue. Bob reminds me of something like that. It feels so familiar but I'm not sure what it is. I start getting nervous and excited when I see him or talk to him. (*She stands up quickly.*) Oh, no! Did I just say *nervous and excited*? I'm not supposed to feel anything at all. What's wrong with me? The Boss *did* send me down here. (*It finally dawns on her.*) Oh, dear, *I'm* the one who is supposed to be here. This so-called mistake isn't about Bob. It's for me! The Boss has sent me back for . . . . unfinished business. But what unfinished business? The accident happened my senior year of high school. (*She thinks hard.*) Right before . . . . *the prom*. Oh, my gosh. I missed my senior prom. I'm here for a reason. (*She pauses.*) I'm the reason. (*She sits back down slowly.*) I get it. Bob Weaver was not on that list because *I* was supposed to come back to earth . . . . and go to the prom. (*She looks up.*) You really do have a sense of humor, Sir. So where is Bob? Oh no, oh no! I've got to find the hospital. He'll be waking up any minute now. (*She quickly exits left.*)

Damian: (*He enters, looks around, and sits down on the ground. Helen catches up and sits next to him.*) I've been looking for you.

Helen: And I've been looking for you, too. I'm tired of all this running around the park.

Damian: Then stop running. (*He sings "It's Gonna Take a Miracle."*)

Helen: I didn't leave *you*! You stopped calling me.

Damian: Every time I called, your mother said you weren't at home. I just assumed you didn't want to see me anymore.

Helen: I was studying chemistry with Irma. You can ask her father. I passed that class because of her.

Damian: I was crazy about you.

Helen: You were?

Damian: Am. I still am. Will you take me back, Helen? Can you forgive me?

Helen: Of course, I will, and I can forgive you. Does that mean we're still going to the prom? (*They laugh and exit with their arms around each other.*)

Angela: (*She comes out from behind the tree and looks up.*) Thank you, sir. It's turning out to be a happy ending for everyone. I wonder if it's too late for me. (*There is a flash of light and then all is darkness.*)

Curtain

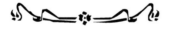

SCENE 3

It's the night of the prom. Angela is dressed in a strapless white gown, looking like an angel. She dances with Bob. Irma and Lester are together, as are Helen and Damian.

Irma: Well, Damian, congratulations on your new job. Just last night Daddy said that you start next week as assistant manager at one of his gas stations.

Damian: Thanks! That's right. And Helen, here, is working the cash register. Hope to see you around.

Irma: Oh, I don't think so. Lester and I have both decided to go to State. I got into nursing school and Lester—he registered late, but he's in! Bob, who's your date? Wow! She looks beautiful. Who is she?

Bob: Oh, sorry. Everyone, this is Angela. She, uh, doesn't live here, so . . . shhh. (*He puts his finger to his mouth.*) She's . . . . she's just visiting for a few days.

Irma: Hi, Angela. I love your dress.

Angela: Oh, thank you. I picked it up at the last minute when Bob asked me to the prom. You might say all of this is (*She looks up.*) . . . . a miracle.

Student announcer: All right, all you guys and gals. It's time for the entertainment you've been waiting for. Bob Weaver and his little band of players have prepared a skit to teach all you cats something about love. (*Laughter erupts and applause. One boy shouts, "What does he know?" Students move back and up stage on a slightly raised platform. Bob and the rest of the cast get into place. Angela moves down left from the crowd and watches from a distance.*)

Bob: Hi, everyone. As you know, Miss Blossom made us read Shakespeare again this year, so we thought we'd put our own spin on the Pyramus and Thisbe part of the play she taught us. I hope that's okay with you, Miss B. (*She waves her hand at him.*) Okay. Well, Barb is going to play the beautiful Thisbe. Jimmy here is going to play the wall with the chink. (*A girl in the audience yells, "Is that cuz he has a hole in his head?" and everyone laughs.*) Sid plays Moonlight, Joe will be the Lion, and I play Pyramus. And that's about it. So, let's begin. (*All move off stage right and left except Jimmy.*)

Wall (Jimmy): I'm a wall and I have a hole in me where the builder forgot to finish building me. But there's this girl and this guy, and their parents won't let them be together, so they meet right here, on either side of me and talk every day. Here comes the boy now.

Pyramus (Bob): Well, here I am. (*He looks through the hole.*) I finally finished my homework so I could meet Thisbe, but where is she? If only we didn't have to meet this way. Hold it! I hear something. (*He looks through the hole again.*) Hey, Baby! What's up?

Thisbe (Barbara): Pyramus, is that you?

Pyramus (Bob): Who else calls you "Baby"?

Thisbe (Barbara): My big handsome Rock, forever and ever.

Pyramus (Bob): And you're my little Doris, now and always in the tunnel of love. Gimme a kiss, baby.

Thisbe (Barbara): Through the hole in this wall. (*They make kissing noises.*)

Pyramus (Bob): Meet me at the carnival on the edge of town. Can you get away now?

Thisbe (Barbara): I'm on my way, sweet thing, come life or death! (*They exit right.*)

Wall (Jimmy): Okay. That's it for me. I'm outa here. (*Wall exits right and Lion and Moonshine enter from left.*)

Lion (Joe): Hi, everyone. I'm an escaped lion—from the zoo up the road, and I'm wild and hairy and really scary. Here comes a girl now. Think I'll scare her.

Moonlight (Sid): And I'm holding this flashlight that's supposed to be moonlight so the girl can see her way through the forest.

Thisbe (Barbara): (*She enters slowly.*) Oh, Pyramus. My darling, Pyramus. I'm here. Baby, where are you? (*Lion leaps out and growls. Thisbe screams and runs away, dropping her letter jacket. The Lion mauls it and exits left. Pyramus enters from right and sees the jacket.*)

Pyramus (Bob): Thisbe? But what's this? It looks like my letter jacket that I asked Thisbe to wear. (*He picks it up and sees it is torn and bloody.*) It is my letter jacket and it has blood on it. Oh, no, my Thisbe is dead, mauled by a lion that escaped from the zoo. How can I live without my darling Thisbe. (*He sits down and sobs into the jacket.*)

Thisbe (Barbara): (*She enters from right and crosses to Pyramus.*) Oh, there you are! Baby, I've been looking everywhere for you. You're not gonna believe this—a lion must have escaped from the zoo, and when I started running, I dropped your jacket. Are you okay?

Sid: Hey, wait a minute. That's not how it ends. Thisbe runs away and Pyramus thinks she's dead and kills himself.

Joe: Yeah, and Thisbe finds him and kills herself, and everyone lives happily ever after.

Barbara: Bob and I decided to change it. (*Moon and Lion look at each other, shrug, and walk off the platform.*)

Bob: Well, folks, I guess that's it for "Pyramus and Thisbe." May all your loves turn out happily ever after. (*The audience applauds while he steps down from the platform, the music continues, and he wanders through the crowd looking for Angela.*) Hey, Jimmy. Did you see my date?

Jimmy: You have a date? When did this miracle happen?

Bob: (*He ignores Jimmy's remark.*) Patti, did you see Angela, the girl in the white dress? We were dancing together before the skit—

Patti: Sorry, Bob. I was dancing with Jimmy, and I didn't have eyes for anyone else. (*She gazes into Jimmy's eyes.*)

Jimmy: That's my girl. (*They begin dancing again, oblivious to Bob.*)

Bob: (*He returns and looks around for her. He walks up to another couple.*) Phil, Alison. You didn't happen to see a pretty girl with a strapless white dress on here tonight?

Alison: That would be half the girls here, Bob. Who is she? Do we know her?

Bob: She's . . . . well, she's . . . . she's an angel. My angel.

Phil: (*He laughs.*) Man, you've got it bad. Good luck finding her. (*They dance away.*)

Bob: (*He finds Angela standing down right watching everyone at the dance.*) Hi, I found you. You look beautiful. Have I told you that already?

Angela: Only about a million times!

Bob: Well, you do. Are you having a good time?

Angela: Yes! I never thought it could happen. But, you know, it can't last forever. When the clock strikes midnight . . . .

Bob: Okay, Cinderella. Now that you're here, you don't really have to go back, do you? Are you playing hard to get, teasing me like this when I've finally found the girl of my dreams? (*He sings "My Special Angel" to her.*) Please say you'll be mine. I love you.

Angela: Bob, you've seen the other side and can understand what I'm about to tell you. It was out of love that I was able to return to earth and have this one last experience.

Bob: What do you mean, one last experience? Aren't you staying?

Angela: No. I can't. My name really *was* on the list, Bob. My being in heaven wasn't a mistake, not like yours. It was out of love for me that I was given the chance to return and go to the senior prom that I missed only a year ago.

Bob: No, this can't be true!

Angela: Bob, please try to understand. I want every minute of this evening to be happy and the time is flying by. When we say goodnight, remember I'll be watching over you. (*They sing a duet of "Goodnight, My Love."*) Now, how about some punch.

Bob: I'll be right back. Stay right there. (*He looks back.*) Don't go away! (*He walks to the other side of the stage to a table with refreshments.*)

Angela: (*She moves down right and looks up.*) I'm ready, Sir. And thank you. Thank you, for everything. I had a really good time. (*She looks over at Bob.*) I'll never forget this night. (*She lifts her arms and the shimmery fabric attached to her dress looks almost like angel's wings. The lights flicker off and she is gone.*)

Bob: (*He returns to the spot where Angela was standing and finds her gone. He looks around with two cups of punch in his hands and stands there. He looks up and then realizes what has happened. It was time for Angela to go.*) I had a feeling this would happen. Saying goodbye was too hard, wasn't it. It was for me, too, Angela. I'll never forget you. (*He must sit down. He walks to some chairs on the side and sits next to a girl who seems to be alone. He looks forlorn. She smiles at him.*)

Liz: Hey, aren't you in my government class? I believe we have four classes together. You've Bob Weaver. I've seen you in all the plays this year. You're really good. (*Bob looks up but is speechless for a moment.*) Oh, I'm Liz.

Bob: (*He can't seem to control his disappointment.*) Oh, ... hi, Liz. Thanks.

Liz: Aren't you having a good time? You sound really down in the dumps.

Bob: (*He tries to recover.*) No, I'm okay. My date had to leave early and I'm all alone now. But thanks for the compliment. I think that definitely excludes the performance tonight, though.

Liz: No, it was good. Happy endings are nice.

Bob: Do you think so?

Liz: Yes, of course. How else would you have it?

Bob: Well, maybe you're right. (*Both are silent for a moment and then he hands her the extra cup of punch.*) Here. You want some punch? (*She takes a cup.*)

Liz: Sure, thanks.

Bob: You wouldn't want to dance with me, would you?

Liz: You . . . . want to dance with me?

Bob: Of course. They're playing my favorite song. Listen—("Love Can Make You Happy" is playing now. He stands up and offers his hand. She smiles, takes it, and they walk to the dance floor. Everyone is dancing. On the final chorus all dancers face the audience, hold hands, and walk down stage singing in a line.)

Final Curtain

Musical Numbers:
Act I
Scene 1
Take Good Care of My Baby. . . . . Regis
    Orig. performed by Bobby Vee, written by Carole King and Gerry Goffin, published by Hal Leonard, 1961

Scene 2
Angel Baby . . . . Irma
    Orig. performed by Rosie and the Originals, written by Rosie Hamlin, Highland Records, 1960
Breaking up Is Hard to Do . . . . Lester
    Orig. performed by Neil Sedaka, written by N. Sedaka & H. Greenfield, RCA Victor Music Group, a unit of BMG Music, 1962

Scene 3
What's Your Name . . . . Bob
    Orig. performed by Don and Juan, written by Claude Johnson and Roland Trone, B-side: "Chicken Necks" 45 RPM, 1961

Pretty Little Angel Eyes . . . . Bob
       Orig. performed by Curtis Lee, written by Tommy Boyce and
       Curtis Lee, Capitol Records, 1961

Act II
Scene 1
One Fine Day . . . . Helen
       Orig. performed by The Chiffons, written by Carole King &
       Gerry Goffin, Screen Gems Dominion Entertainment, 1963
Devoted to You . . . . Bob and Irma
       Orig. performed by The Everly Brothers, written by
       Boudleaux Bryant, Bryant Publications, Barnaby Records, Ace
       Music Service, 1958

Scene 2
Blue Moon . . . . Angela
       Orig. performed by The Marcels, written by Richard Rogers
       & Lorenz Hart, MGM, 1934
It's Gonna Take a Miracle . . . . Damian
       Orig. performed by The Royalettes, written by Teddy Randazzo
       with Bobby Weinstein and Lou Stallman, MGM, 1965

Scene 3
My Special Angel. . . . . Bob
       Orig. performed by Bobby Helms, written by Jimmy Duncan,
       MCA Records, 1963
Goodnight, My Love. . . . . Bob and Angela
       Orig. performed by Jesse Belvin, written by G. Mendola and
       Macascalco, Virgin Records America, 1956
Love Can Make You Happy . . . . Bob and the Cast
       Orig. performed by Mercy, written by J. Sigler, Jamie Music
       Publishing Co., 1969

The Gentle Art of Reappearing

On the island of Galveston off the coast of Texas, Bill Prosper runs a magic shop called The Tempest, which he inherited from his father. When his father died, Bill's brother Anthony abandoned Bill and his sister to pursue a more glamorous career. Now three years later he appears at the shop unannounced, having accompanied the great entertainment magnate Vince King on business. It is the island's annual Christmas festival, and King has brought in the rock band Storm as the main attraction.

What happens next parallels Shakespeare's last play *The Tempest*. Two brothers reunite but not until the magic pranks of a spirit named Ariel have taken their toll on the characters in this haunted Victorian setting. All's well in the end when Miranda and Vince's son Freddie get together. The entire group flies off to Los Angeles for a holiday, leaving The Tempest in the capable hands of Bill's assistant Cal.

In reality, acts of reconciliation are difficult. Loss and recovery, what we refer to as death and rebirth in archetypal symbolism, exact a painful price. As Shakespeare proves time and again, however, the redemptive power of love is the magic ingredient necessary for the gentle art of reappearing.

Synopsis of Scenes:

Act I
Scene 1: A magic shop called The Tempest on the Strand in Galveston, midmorning on a cold December day
Scene 2: The Tempest later that day
Scene 3: The Tempest that afternoon
Scene 4: The Tempest that evening

Act II

Scene 1: The Tempest the next morning
Scene 2: The Tempest, Saturday afternoon
Scene 3: The Tempest around five in the afternoon
Scene 4: The Tempest Sunday morning
Scene 5: The Tempest Monday morning

Characters:

Bill Prosper: Owner of The Tempest, a young man in his twenties
Ariel: A teenage girl turned into a ghost by her evil mother who then disappeared
Toby: Lead singer for the famous rock band Storm
Anthony: Bill's younger brother and assistant to entertainment magnate Vince King
Gonzales: Assistant to Anthony and longtime friend to Bill
Vince: President of King Entertainment Group, Inc.
Ferdinand (Freddie): Vince's teenage son
Cal: A shy teenage boy who works at The Tempest
Miranda: Bill's younger sister
Mary: Manager of The Mariner
Three Customers

ACT 1

SCENE 1

    Dim lights come up on Ariel and Bill looking into a magic crystal ball. Then lights come up on four men as they enter, three in heavy coats and one in a black leather jacket, a gold scarf and sun glasses. The wind is howling. It is clearly a cold, blustery day, atypical of this small island off the Texas coast, but it is a December that apparently has ignored the notion of global warming. The air is frigid. Vince King, president of King Entertainment Group, Inc. and the decision maker of the group, normally does not accompany the musicians he represents on their tours, but he has made a quick detour from his winter vacation in Miami in order to attend the island's famous annual Dickens style Christmas festival. He enters later in the scene. His son Ferdinand, known by friends and family as Freddie, is being groomed by his father as the future head of the company. Anthony, who is Bill and Miranda's estranged brother, works for Vince. Gonzales tags along as an aid to Anthony. The center of attention is Toby, lead singer for the currently popular rock band called Storm. His shades, his swaggering step, his black leather jacket and tight pants, and the gold lame scarf around his neck betray his calling as well as his attitude about life. It is midmorning on this cold December day.

Toby: Dudes. Why are we waiting here? Look at me, man. I'm out on the pavement. I'm freezing to death, man. Not only do I not have time for this, my vocal chords are gonna snap any minute. Who's important here, I ask you. (*No response.*) Anybody? How 'bout you, An tony and Cle o patra? Huh?

Anthony: Look, Toby. I've told you three times. Vince and Freddie are buying a present for Vince's wife. We were supposed to meet them here. I'm sure they'll be out any minute.

Toby: Yeah, well, you said that twenty minutes ago. In a minute he's not gonna have a lead singer, and then what's he gonna do, huh? Contract don't say nothin' about freezin' my—

Gonzales: Yeah, he's right, Tony. Maybe we should find a coffee shop and get something hot to drink. I could use some defrosting myself. We've been standing here for over thirty minutes.

(Vince and Freddie finally emerge with packages in each hand, Christmas wrapping spilling over the tops of the bulging shopping bags.)

Vince: Terrific shop! Great PR! They've got these young salesgirls dressed to the nines handing out little cups of hot chocolate while customers look around. And they had these little pastries and stuff and chocolate cookies with silver icing. My wife would go nuts over this place. *(All look at him in silence and disbelief as they stand before him shivering. He gets it.)* Okay. Ready to go?

Freddie: *(He removes a slip of paper from his pocket.)* It looks like this is the street. 3618, that would be, I think, right next to that coffee shop over there. The name on the shop should say The Tempest.

Anthony: Yeah, that's it. *(He stares at it with unusual concentration.)*

Toby: You guys get the smoke blower. I'm getting outa here. My ears are starting to burn, dude. *(He turns toward the street off right.)* TAXI! *(He exits.)*

Vince: *(Pulling his coat collar up on his neck.)* Brrr! It's cold out here. I thought you said it never gets this cold here in December. *(Anthony and Gonzales look at each other and back at Vince. They quickly exit stage left.)*

Curtain

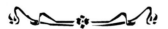

Scene 2

Cal is working his shift at the little magic shop in the old Victorian section of the island that has been preserved by its inhabitants. He is a teenage boy who doesn't seem to grasp the concept of grooming and furthermore isn't bothered by it. His hair darts out in several directions and he sees the world through thick black framed lenses. Even with glasses he can't see Ariel, the ghost who inhabits the shop, but he can hear her and he can detect her presence with increasing irritation.

Cal: *(Ariel uses a stick to poke him in the ribs.)* Ow! That hurt! Stop it, Ariel. *(She pokes him again.)* Enough! I mean it this time. If you don't cut it out, I'm going to tell Bill and THEN you'll be sorry.

Ariel: Tattle-tale. I'm just having a little fun. Can't you take a joke?

Cal: *(Ariel moves items as he reaches for them.)* Fun? Fun for you, maybe. Buzz off, you little fly. I have work to do. Since you seem to be able to see everything, you'd know that. *(He begins to arrange items on a shelf and talk more to himself than to Ariel.)* Crowds are going to be pouring in soon. It's one of our busiest seasons.

Ariel: Oh, where's your sense of humor? You're getting to be such a drag. Besides, I'm bored. You were much more fun when you were younger.

Cal: Younger? I've only been working here a year.

Ariel: And what a difference a year can make.

Cal: *(He turns around sharply to face where he thinks she is.)* Well, someone around here has to work. Look at this place.

Ariel: Ugh! I hate this drafty old, cramped pitiful excuse for living. Do you know what it's like to be taken prisoner by Italian, Chinese, and Mexican food drifting through these walls at the same time several hours a day? You're at school, but I KNOW. I'm stuck here thinking about food all day. (*She slumps in a chair near him.*) My brain is becoming addicted to food additives. So quit whining about your tiny little troubles. I'm ready to get out and have some fun for a change. (*He drags a box over to her chair to sit down and unpack a shipment, unaware that Ariel is in that chair. She shoves him out.*) Hey!

Cal: Oops. Sorry. Make up your mind. I never know where you are. You just make yourself at home wherever you feel like it.

Ariel: Yeah, yeah. You'd better make up your mind to watch where you're parking it, buddy. Anyway, I live here, and it's not like I have a choice.

Cal: (*Cal feels the air to make sure she isn't in the chair.*) You know what, *you* need to watch it. You need to start behaving yourself, or you're going to be around for my grandchildren's grandchildren. As I recall, (*She takes the tinsel out the box and wraps it around him while he brushes it aside.*) rumor has it that The Tempest was shut down by the city for bizarre "incidents" that you seem to have been responsible for, and your mother made you permanently invisible before disappearing herself.

Ariel: (*She snaps back at him.*) Not permanently. Bill and I have . . . . an agreement.

Cal: Uh-huh. You couldn't hold up your end of an agreement with glue on your fingers. I know what you're thinking. If you perform some charitable act of goodness for him, he'll set you free. Well, think again, bumble bee. Bill has a happy life, now that his brother's out of the picture. He keeps busy looking after his sister, who turned out to be pretty nice. (*Ariel turns to him and snarls with a look of jealousy.*) So, why would he ever need your help, you little insect. (*He ducks as a book comes flying toward him.*)

Ariel: Oo—oo-h, you-u-u! I'll get you! Besides, how'd you know all that stuff about his brother?

Cal: I have ears. And I pay attention. Now, go away. I'm a busy man.

Ariel: Ha! *Man!* You're just a punk kid who can't get a real job. (*She pinches him.*)

Cal: Ow! (*He swings a broom at her, but she's already on the other side of the room.*)

Ariel: Ha, ha! Missed me! (*She taps him on the head and runs away.*)

Cal: Be glad I can't see you, hornet brain. (*He puts the broom down and resumes working.*)

Ariel: That's more like it. I love it when you talk insect. (*She puts antennae on her head.*) Just be careful you don't get stung. (*She goes after him with her stinger finger, but then settles down in a comfy chair again and drapes one leg over the arm, pleased with her own bit of humor.*) Oh, come on. Things aren't always what they seem.

Cal: (*He is looking up slowly at her bobbing antennae headband.*) You do know I can see where you are with that ridiculous thing on your head. (*She throws the headband on the floor and moves to another chair.*) Wait a minute. Do you know something I don't know? (*He walks slowly to where he thinks she is standing.*)

Ariel: Uh, over here, big guy. (*He turns to face her but looks above her head.*) Down here.

Cal: Okay. Give it up. What do you know, and does Bill need to know it?

Ariel: *(She gets up and walks to the bookshelf, Cal unaware of her change in position.)* Let's just say a storm may be heading this way.

(Bill and Miranda enter the shop. Bill is carrying a box.)

Bill: *(He is finishing a conversation with Miranda.)* Great. If you'll check the contents with the invoices, Cal can get this on the shelves as soon as possible. We don't have much time, but this could be the boost in sales we need.

Miranda: I'll get right on it. Hi, Cal. Shop looks good.

Cal: Hi, Miranda. Thanks. It hasn't been easy. Ran into a few glitches. *(Ariel bops him on the head with a book, which he catches.)* Ow!

Miranda: Cal, what just happened?

Cal: Uh, it's . . . . nothing. Book fell off the shelf. *(He rubs his head and scowls, looking around for Ariel.)*

Miranda: *(She looks at the shelf.)* Hmm. That's odd. I restocked that shelf yesterday, but . . . . I don't remember any loose books. They were all packed pretty tight. *(She stares at the shelves puzzled.)*

Cal: Oh, don't worry. I must've backed into it. I'm okay. Really. Need some help unpacking boxes?

Bill: *(He has just entered from the back room.)* Actually, Cal, would you mind going across the street for some more tape and staples? *(He hands him a five.)*

Cal: Okay, sure. *(He exits through the shop door.)*

Miranda: *(She takes a wreath out of a box and places it on the door.)* That's better.

Bill: Nice touch. You're good with things like that. Must have gotten that from Mom.

Miranda: *(She begins humming a Christmas carol.)* I love this time of year, even if it does make me a little sad.

Bill: What is this frown? You're the cheerful one. I'm counting on you. Hey, we have a good life. I've got the business and you'll be going to college in a couple of years. Life's okay. Help me put this up. *(He hands her the tinsel. He's going to tape it to the counter. She arranges it for him.)* Here? *(She nods and he tapes.)* I wonder who the entertainment's going to be this year at the Rose. I've been too busy to notice. Has it even been announced?

Miranda: Actually, it has. It's that terrific group called Storm, and . . . . Shane asked me to go with him. He got tickets.

Bill: Shane. Not that Shane that works as a busboy down the street at The Mariner? *(She nods, somewhat fearful of his response.)* You're kidding, right?

Miranda: *(She turns away from Bill.)* No. He's okay and . . . . *(She turns to face him)* I really want to go. It's just a concert. And . . . . Bill, you can't keep acting like my father. I'm old enough to go out with guys, even though I never do. Besides, I do okay in school, don't I? I help you every day in the shop. I never get in trouble for ANYTHING. Everybody I know thinks I'm a goody-goody. Translate *boring.* I can guess what they say behind my back. Bill, I really want to go. It's Christmas and—

Bill: *(He is resigning himself to it.)* Okay. You're right, as usual. I just feel like I have to protect you all the time. I'm all you've got, you know.

Miranda: And you're a great older brother. *(She hugs him gleefully.)* I'm going to be fine. It's Christmas and I feel like singing. *(She turns on the radio to Christmas music and begins humming and singing along while she decorates a tree up center. Bill joins her. Cal comes in with four cups from Starbucks and a bag of tape and staples.)* Cal, thanks! This is perfect. *(He hands out the cups and leaves the fourth cup in the holder, looking around the room for Ariel, not realizing that he is actually looking right at her. He picks up the cup and Ariel takes it from him, somewhat startled at his generous gesture. The three toast each other, and with Miranda's back to her, Ariel, too, raises her cup. Cal alone watches Ariel's cup rise and he pauses. He looks straight at Ariel and she knows it.)*

Cal: *(He raises his cup, looking at Ariel.)* To friends.

Curtain

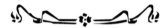

SCENE 3

The Tempest is empty when Vince, Anthony, Freddie, and Gonzales enter the shop. A holiday bell tinkles as they enter. Cal enters through a beaded curtain separating the shop from a storage room. Ariel is sitting comfortably reading a book.

Ariel: 'Bout time. I came close to using a really wicked spell to make them go away.

Cal: *(He ignores her.)* Welcome to The Tempest. May I help you?

Anthony: Yes, that is, I hope so. *(He looks around as if searching for something or someone. He then hands Cal a business card.)* I represent Vin—a, uh, certain group of entertainers who will be needing a visual effect. It's a last minute decision, that is, actually the people I represent are in need of a device for creating smoke or fog on stage. Can you help me?

Cal: Not too many requests for that kind of thing. We're not really into supplies for performing arts. But there was this fraternity last year that ordered a fog machine for a Halloween party. I'll have to ask my boss. (*Freddie and Gonzales begin to look around the shop, intrigued with its contents. Ariel, still sitting in the chair, looks at them warily.*)

Anthony: All right. (*He stands at the counter waiting.*)

Cal: Uh, you may not want to wait, unless you have a couple of hours to kill. He won't be back until about three.

Anthony: Oh, right. Actually, if he could give me a call as soon as possible, I'd appreciate it. We're staying at the Seaside. (*He hands him his card.*)

Cal: Sure. (*He reads the card.*) No problem. Anthony Prosper. Unusual name. You don't have a brother, do you?

Anthony: (*He looks at him for a moment without answering.*) I used to. (*He looks over at Freddie.*) Hey, Freddie. We need to get going.

Freddie: Well, willya look at this! I can't believe it. See all these dragons. I loved these things when I was a kid. I actually had one that was eight feet tall. I used to scare my friends with it. See, I had this dragon with his arm raised and his mouth wide open showing these vicious looking teeth—like he was gonna eat me up.

Ariel: Too bad he didn't.

Cal: (*He gives her a frown.*) Be nice.

Freddie: Oh. No, I didn't really mean that about my friends . . . .

Cal: Sorry. Not you. I was just talking to . . . . the witch. (*He points to the chair where Ariel is sitting and she pretends to be offended.*)

Freddie: There's no one sitting . . . . oh, I get it. One of your little gimmicks to create the ambiance of magic, eh?

Cal: Actually, it's just a joke we have about the shop. You know, "haints and hot steams," witches and dragons, "bubble, bubble, toil and trouble."

Ariel: Now you're talkin'! I could use some bubble, bubble. It's freezing in here. Can't you throw a few logs on the fire, or turn up the thermostat or something? (*Cal looks straight at Freddie as if he has heard nothing.*)

Anthony: (*He grabs Freddie and Gonzales.*) Well, uh, thanks very much for your help. We'll be in touch. (*They exit.*)

Cal: Okay, that's it! No more playing up when customers come in. One of these days Bill is going to find out and I'm gonna get the boot—you, too, if you're not careful.

Ariel: Not careful? That's exactly what I do want. Don't you get it? I'm stuck here. Even when I run his ridiculous errands for him, I'm forced to come back to this dump. That spell that dear old Mum cast says I have to perform "feats of selfless heroism for the benefit of mankind." Yeah, right. Like I care about mankind. Besides, what did mankind ever do for me? Even if I wanted to, how is that supposed to happen on this island in this crummy little shop? I'm going to die of boredom if I don't get outa here. Then you'll have a dead ghost on your hands. A dead ghost. Now that's an interesting concept. I wonder if it's something like a zombie—

Cal: You need to chill or something. Have you been into the chocolate covered cherries again? Maybe you should go take a nap and sleep it off.

Ariel: Ugh! Why does everyone want me to sleep? I need adventure. I NEED A LIFE! (*She goes into the back room to sulk.*)

(*Bill and Miranda enter.*)

Miranda: Hi, Cal. I'll take over the inventory now. (*She goes through the beaded curtain and into the back room.*)

Bill: Hey, Cal. Business pick up yet? (*He leans in to speak quietly to Cal.*) Where's Ariel?

Cal: (*He looks around for Ariel, even though he can't see her.*) She's not here? Good. I told her to go take a nap and chill. She was getting seriously out of control with her "I'm bored out of my mind" routine again, and you know what that means. Can't you find something useful for her to do? She's driving me crazy. Oh, by the way (*He hands Bill Anthony's business card*), these guys in suits came by looking for a fog machine. I told 'em about the one you sold to that fraternity last year for a Halloween party, but I said you . . . . wouldn't . . . . be . . . . Hey, is everything okay?

Bill: Well, well, whadya know. After all this time, he shows up here, at The Tempest, wanting my help.

Cal: You know this guy?

Bill: You could say that. Miranda and I had . . . . have an older brother, Cal. It's a long story, but the short of it is this. He decided his career with his band was more important than keeping the family together. My father ran this shop for years before he died—all of this, even the ghosts and spirits of the past. It was overwhelming. I was barely eighteen and

Miranda was twelve. It was all I could do to keep our heads above water. We needed his help, but he didn't see it that way and left. That was three years ago. So now he wants *my* help. How ironic. I wonder what he's doing here.

Cal: So that guy *was* your brother? Why didn't he say so? Wait a minute. I looked at the name on his card and when I asked if he had a brother, thinking he might know you, he said *he used to.*

Bill: I guess he didn't want you asking too many questions. I don't know. I'm not even sure why he would bother to come here. The more I think about it, the more I'd like to punch him. Who does he think he is, waltzing in here unannounced after three years of silence? We didn't even know where he was. (*Getting up angry*) Where's Ariel? (*He goes into the back room as Miranda comes out.*)

Miranda: Cal, have you seen the invoice for Dragons, Etc.? I seem to have misplaced it.

Cal: No, I haven't, but it might be under the counter there. Bill was looking at it earlier. (*She goes to look.*)

(*Bill crosses to chair DL with Ariel in tow. She has the wand in her hand. Miranda is sitting on a stool behind the counter looking through a stack of papers. Bill, takes the wand from Ariel, mumbles a few words and points the wand at Miranda, who suddenly drops her head to the counter and sleeps.*)

Cal: Ouch! She's gonna feel *that* when she wakes up.

Bill: (*He affectionately pats Miranda's head.*) Sorry 'bout that, little sis, but I need to talk to Ariel. You're better off not knowing about her. (*He crosses to Ariel and pulls up a stool.*) Ariel, I need your help. (*She mouths "Moi?"*) I heard you're bored.

Ariel: You can say that again.

Bill: I have a task for you.

Ariel: Name it! I'll do anything to get out of here.

Bill: My brother Anthony was here today.

Ariel: Which one was Anthony? I didn't see a scruffy-looking, long-haired, unkempt little weasel. Did I miss something?

Bill: (*Ignoring her gibes*) He's cleaned up his act. Apparently he works for the great entertainment magnate Vince King out in Los Angeles now.

Ariel: Never heard of him.

Bill: You may not know the name Vince King, but you've heard of Storm, right?

Ariel: *The* Storm? As in (*She begins singing and moving her hips.*) *Baby, baby, you're rippin' my heart in two? That* Storm? Sure. Everybody's heard of Storm.

Bill: Well, they're playing the Christmas concert this year and Vince King represents them. That's why he and his staff are on the island now.

Ariel: Are you getting ready to tell me that I'm gonna get to meet the lead singer of Storm? Oh, great one, make my day. PLEASE, make my day. (*She gets on her knees and bows to Bill.*)

Bill: Not exactly. (*She gets up.*)

Ariel: What then?

Bill: Remember that trick you did back in July when you made the oysters on my plate sprout arms and legs and start dancing on their half shells?

Ariel: (*Smiling*) Yeah, that was definitely one of my better days. You nearly peed in your pants.

Bill: I want you to do it again.

Ariel: (*She frowns at him.*) Hey, you're not getting masochistic on me, are you? Once wasn't enough for you, huh, buddy?

Bill: No, no. I want you to find Anthony and his partners and give 'em the scare of their lives. We're talking Golden Globe—

Ariel: Finally! Something to live for . . . (*She looks at Cal, flicks his ear and laughs. He winces and swings. She ducks.*) . . . besides torturing Cal.

Bill: Okay, you two. Knock it off.

Cal: Me! One of these days I'm gonna get that little viper and then she'll wish she'd never looked at me!

Ariel: Aw, what happened to flying insect imagery? I'm so disappointed, and (*feigning fear but sarcastically*) o-oh, I'm shakin' and quakin' cause you're really scarin' me. Look, buddy, boy. You should thank me. If it weren't for my magic, you wouldn't even *hear* me. I'm an improvement in your pathetic little socially challenged life.

Bill: (*He snaps his finger in front of her face.*) Try to concentrate, will you. I need for you to go now and keep an eye on them. Encourage them, in your own unique way, to dine at The Mariner. It's sure to have the largest dinner crowd tonight. (*He sits back, relaxing a little.*) I think it might do him good to experience some pain, and the more public it is, the better.

Ariel: Pain? (*Getting excited*) Now you're talking'! Just how painful *are* we talking?

Bill: (*He sits up quickly.*) NO! No sneezing, coughing, choking, or eyes rolling. And NO BLOOD! Just the dancing oysters. Anything else and you've bought permanent residence here. Eternity. Got it? I don't want to give him a heart attack. Just make him feel some discomfort. Can you do that?

Ariel: Oh, all right. You're such a poop. (*She turns back to face him.*) Not even one little sneezing spell?

Bill: No. Now get going.

Ariel: (*She starts for the door and turns to look at Cal.*) Bye, cutie. You're so gonna miss me when I'm gone. (*Cal throws a pillow at the door and she laughs as she ducks to miss it.*)

Curtain

Scene 4: *Cal and Miranda are in the shop alone restocking, cleaning, and getting the shelves and products organized. Freddie enters the shop alone. He has returned to purchase the small dragon figurine he saw earlier, when he hears Miranda singing along with the holiday music on the radio.*

Cal: Hi. Come back for the dragon? Good idea. They're going fast for Christmas. One of our most popular items.

Freddie: That girl . . . . her voice . . . . it's beautiful, like an angel. Does she work here? (*Miranda goes into the back room.*)

Cal: Oh, that's Miranda. Yeah. She and her brother own this shop. And she's always singing. Makes it nice to work here. (*He yells toward the back.*) Hey, Miranda! Can you come out here for a minute?

Miranda: What's up? (*She sees Freddie, straightens her posture a bit, and stares at him, a smile slowly forming on her mouth.*) Hello.

Freddie: Hello.

Cal: This is Miranda and this is . . . . (*Neither one looks at Cal but stares at each other.*) I'm sorry. I didn't get your name.

Freddie: (*He looks straight at Miranda.*) Ferdinand King . . . . Freddie. Everyone just calls me Freddie.

Miranda: Hi, Freddie. I saw you looking at the dragons. Are you a collector?

Freddie: Oh, no. Not really. I had one when I was a kid, though. It was great. For an eight year old, it was powerful. And terrifying. I loved it.

Miranda: So, do you still love powerful and terrifying things? I'm afraid you're in the wrong place if you do. Everything here is make believe. (*She laughs.*) If you want scary, try watching the news. That's good for a few nightmares.

Freddie: Well, you could be right about that. (*He picks up the dragon again and stares at it.*)

Miranda: Would you like me to wrap that up for you?

Freddie: Why not? It brings back great memories, and maybe I could start a new one. Like, coming into this shop one Christmas when I found a dragon and met an angel.

Miranda: (*He looks up quickly and down again, blushing. She moves to the counter smiling.*) That's one I haven't heard before.

Freddie: I heard you singing. You have an amazing voice. Have you ever sung for an audience?

Miranda: (*Laughing*) Of course. I think I was in third grade. It was Presidents Day and I was a singing rabbit in Martha Washington's garden.

Freddie: Wow, a singing rabbit.

Miranda: I love to sing. *For myself.* It makes me feel . . . . content. It's the best way I know to pass the time and make myself feel better about things. I'm not sure I'd feel that way if I had to sing on command.

Freddie: But you could be famous with a voice like that.

Miranda: Famous, huh? America's Got Talent, right? Why would I want to be famous? Besides, the shop keeps me pretty busy, and I'll be applying to colleges next year.

Freddie: You friend here tells me you run this shop with your brother.

Miranda: Yes, that's right. We have for the last three years.

Freddie: I came in the shop yesterday, but you weren't here.

Miranda: Oh, really? Why didn't you get the dragon then? Were you undecided?

Freddie: I can't tell you what made me come in here today. It was as if I were being drawn by some strange force. It sounds weird, I know. But I can't explain it. Maybe there really is magic in this shop. Is that what you guys do here, cast spells on people? Yesterday, however, I was on a mission, looking for a fog machine that the technical guys forgot. My dad manages the rock group that's performing tonight for the island's annual Christmas celebration.

Miranda: But I thought Storm was the entertainment this year.

Freddie: That's right. Hey, why don't you go with me tonight?

Miranda: Is this some kind of joke?

Freddie: Oh, no! I mean it. Seriously. I'd really like for you to join us. Be my date.

Miranda: (*She appears at a loss for words, stammering and hesitating.*) I . . . . I . . . . I'm afraid I . . . . You're kidding, right?

Freddie: How about it? Is seven okay?

Miranda: No, no, I'm sorry. I actually have a date for the concert, but thanks for asking.

Freddie: Well, then, if you won't go to the concert with me, come to Los Angeles for an audition. Once my father hears you sing, he'll agree. You have the voice of an angel.

(*Bill enters through the door of the shop, returning from an errand. Ariel follows him in and escapes to the back room.*)

Bill: (*He looks at Freddie and nods.*) Good afternoon.

Miranda: Bill, this is Freddie King. His father manages Storm!

Bill: Weren't you guys looking for a fog machine earlier? I tried to call him back but got no answer.

Freddie: That's okay. I think they changed their minds. That's Toby for you.

Bill: (*Interested*) I see. Well, you've got a busy night tonight, don't you. I hear the concert is sold out.

Freddie: That's right. I invited your sister to be our guest, but it seems she's already one of the fortunate ticket holders.

Bill: I'm not so sure about the fortunate part, but she's pretty excited about seeing Storm.

Freddie: Maybe you'd like to be our guest. I have extra tickets if you'd—

Bill: That's very generous of you, but no. I've got to be here early in the morning to open the shop. But thanks, anyway. (*He turns to get back to work.*)

Freddie: I, uh, heard Miranda singing when I came in. She really ought to do something with that voice, let the whole world hear her. I think she should let my dad hear her sing when we get back to LA. She's extraordinary.

Bill: I'm afraid that's not possible.

Miranda: Wait! You forgot your dragon. (*He turns back toward her and holds on to the dragon as does Miranda. They look at each other, reluctant to let go. Miranda releases it and he starts for the door. But Ariel has entered with the wand in her hand. She mumbles a few words, pointing at Freddie first, and then Miranda, and watches.*)

Miranda: Wait! (*Freddie turns around.*) Do you play chess? (*She crosses to a lovely old chess game set out on a table down left.*)

Freddie: Yes. Yes, I do! But I warn you. I'm very good.

Miranda: (*She pulls up another chair for Freddie.*) Up to the challenge? No time like the present.

Curtain

ACT II

Scene 1: *The scene opens with the Oyster Ballet. The stage is dark. French cabaret music comes up and five actors in black enter from left with glow-in-the-dark oyster shells attached to their black gloves. When the black light comes on, the gloved actors make the glowing oysters do a little dance and then exit right. When the lights come on, it is Saturday morning. Two customers are paying for items at the register. Anthony enters and bides his time, looking at books and decorative items for sale. The couple leaves and Anthony turns around.*

Bill: May I help—(*Bill sees it is his brother Anthony.*)

Anthony: Hello.

Bill: It's you.

Anthony: Yeah, it's me.

Bill: Cal gave me your card. Said you were looking for a smoke machine.

Anthony: Yeah, well. Somehow the band's got left behind with another piece of equipment and they threatened to cancel if we didn't come up with another one.

Bill: So, no concert?

Anthony: (*Smiling*) Nah. Vince pacified them with another sweet deal.

Bill: Oh, okay . . . . was there anything else?

Anthony: Well . . . . I had a really interesting experience at The Mariner last night, a sign perhaps. I was hoping we could talk.

Bill: Why?

Anthony: What do you mean *why*? Last time I checked we were still brothers.

Bill: Is that right. (*He turns back to his paper work.*) No one around here noticed. The only family I've had any contact with is right here on this island. You do remember you have a sister named Miranda?

Anthony: Okay. What do you want me to do? I messed up, okay. I said it. Do you want me to grovel?

Bill: That would be a new twist, but somehow I just can't picture the up and coming entertainment mogul groveling.

Anthony: When did you become so righteous? Mr. Perfect, the one without blame, the martyr who left his dreams on the curb?

Bill: You gave me no choice. You took your share of the money Dad left and then disappeared. Talk about magic. We had no idea where you were. We could've used your help getting the shop back on its feet—the books were a mess, but more than that, we needed to act like a family. Miranda needed it more than anyone.

Anthony: I had dreams. I couldn't stick around and just watch them die. I had to grab my chance when I could. I'm not the one who gets second chances.

Bill: Right. Well, you made your decision. We weren't part of it, so don't think you can just walk through that door and act like nothing's happened.

Anthony: So that's it? That's all you can say?

Bill: I don't believe you, man. There's nothing else to say. Look, we don't need you or your help. You might as well go back to LA and let us all move on without reopening this thing.

Anthony: This *thing*? You haven't changed. Still self-righteous as ever. The stone face with a stone heart. I was a fool to think you were capable of understanding or even forgiving. (*He walks toward the door, waiting for Bill to stop him. Bill remains silent and Anthony leaves. Bill looks around the shop, gets up, picks up a book, throws it across the floor, and then sits in a chair with his head in his hands. Miranda enters from the outside, takes her coat off, and hangs it on the coat rack.*)

Miranda: (*She looks around the shop and spots Bill looking forlorn.*) Oh, dear. It looks like the manager from The Mariner already paid you a visit. Are they suing us?

Bill: (*He looks up confused from his descent into depression.*) What?

Miranda: Shane said there was something weird going on at one of the tables last night—something about the food. I couldn't quite get the whole picture, but apparently one of the customers began yelling about oysters dancing on the table. Bit too much to drink, I suppose. Then all of a sudden the table fell over and people began fighting. When it was all over, one of the men at the table told the manager he heard this hissy voice repeating, "Bill's Revenge! Bill's Revenge!"

Bill: A *sissy* voice?

Miranda: What? No, I said *hissy* voice. You know, hissing, like a snake.

Bill: Oh. So this hissy voice repeated *my* name?

Miranda: Yes, listen. I'm trying to tell you what happened. Anyway, the voice began cackling like a witch. The man who paid the bill said he was certain the voice meant *Bill Prosper*. When Shane told me, I couldn't stop laughing. Have you ever heard anything so ridiculous in all your life?

Bill:　(*Sitting back down, he slumps into the chair with an arm over his eyes.*) I'm having a nightmare and when I wake up it will all just disappear.

Miranda: Wait a minute. You didn't know anything about this?

Bill:　(*Still hiding his face, eyes closed*) More or less.

Miranda: Oh. (*She sits for a moment in silence.*)

Bill:　(*Opening his eyes.*) Okay. Are they suing me, or what? What'd you find out?

Miranda: Nothing. You're not taking this seriously, are you? It's nothing. Just a party that got out of hand. Cheer up. (*She starts singing.*)

Bill:　No singing. Not now. (*He pauses.*) Anthony came by.

Miranda: Anthony? *Our* Anthony? (*She squeals with delight and runs to him.*) Where is he? Is he all right? When's he coming back?

Bill:　(*Raising his voice, he gets up and crosses over to the work area.*) He's not coming back. So don't ask and stop wondering. When are you going to get it through your thick skull, Miranda? He abandoned us. He took the money and ran—walked out on us when we needed help because he cares about one person—himself. The sooner you grow up and accept that, the sooner we can get on with our lives. (*Miranda has now begun to sob. He is suddenly sad to see her upset.*) Aw, don't cry. I'm sorry. Miranda, please stop crying. I don't know what came over me. (*He sits beside her.*) Temporary insanity. Pent up hostility. I'm tired and Anthony makes me crazy. I'm weary of holding it all together. (*Miranda mumbles something.*) What's that?

Miranda: (*Sobbing, she sits up.*) I said how could you send him away? What is it with you two? Why couldn't you just make up and be friends so we can be a family again? What good is this stubborn pride when all it does is make you both miserable, and me, too?

Bill: I was eighteen years old, Miranda! Our father was dying. When Anthony left I was the one in charge. He was older—he should have been the one to stay. Suddenly I was supposed to be the adult in charge. *Take care of the store, Bill. Watch over your little sister, Bill. Pay the bills, make ends meet, send Miranda to college. No sweat. You'll be okay.* Well, I wasn't. I was scared out of my mind. Every day for the past three years I've thought just one day at a time. I'm afraid to imagine what's going to happen beyond that. What if I screw up, get sick, forget to lock up one night? Make one little slip, and it all disappears.

Miranda: *You* were afraid? You? I . . . . but you're always so calm and sure about everything.

Bill: Right. I guess I fake it pretty well, huh.

Miranda: (*Sobbing again*) Oh, Bill. I'm sorry. I've been so selfish.

Bill: No, you haven't. (*Comforting her*) You've been great. So easy to talk to and cheerful, always singing those stupid little songs. You have a calming effect on me. (*He puts his arm around her.*)

Miranda: (*Looking up at him*) Forgive him, Bill. Ask him to come back. I need him in my life. *We* need him. (*Looking under the counter, she retrieves a business card and holds it up.*) I'm going to find him, Bill. (*Pulling on her coat*) He has to come back and you have to tell him to. (*She runs out without a protest from him.*)

Curtain

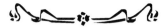

Scene 2: *It is Saturday afternoon and Bill is sitting at the counter doing paper work. Ariel is flopped out in the big chair with spirits sitting on either side of her—two young women dressed in flowing white gowns, new arrivals in the shop. Miranda walks in and slowly hangs up her coat.*

Bill: Fresh coffee.

Miranda: No, thanks.

Bill: Tea? Cal brought some chai this . . . .

Miranda: No.

Bill: You didn't find him?

Miranda: Oh, yes. I found him.

Bill: Well?

Miranda: His exact words were, "He can rot in—"

Bill: Okay, okay. I know the rest. It figures. See, I was right. Now do you understand what I'm talking about?

Miranda: Truly mature behavior, from both of you. I'm going to take a nap. (*She exits behind the beaded curtain.*)

Ariel: (*Waking up from her nap in the big chair, she stretches noisily. The two spirits stretch, too.*) I feel just like a cat who's been out all night. Ooo—what a night! Made a couple of friends, too. Said they could crash here. What's happening?

Bill: Not much.

Ariel: Must be a slow day. No annoying customers.

Bill: Nope, not many. (*He avoids eye contact with her.*)

Ariel: Okay. (*She walks toward him.*) I, uh, guess you heard about last night.

Bill: I'm just waiting for the other shoe to drop. Which version are you going to tell me?

Ariel: (*Enthusiastic*) Well, you told me to give 'em a good scare, so I did. You should have seen the look on their faces when the oysters began sprouting legs. If that isn't worthy of my freedom, nothing is.

Bill: (*Detached*) And then what happened?

Ariel: Nothin' much. You know, one or two other insignificant little things.

Bill: How insignificant?

Ariel: All right! So the manager was a little upset.

Bill: Upset?

Ariel: And threatening to sue you.

Bill: Sue me? Why would she think I had anything to do with it?

Ariel: (*Looking away*) I'm never getting outa here, am I? I'm doomed to this shallow existence, confined like a prisoner to these four walls forever and ever. (*She slumps into a chair.*) It's existentialism for real, like that John Paul something-something wrote. I'm in a living hell.

Bill: If you just hadn't yelled out my name over and over—"Bill's revenge! Bill's revenge!"

Ariel: Oh, that. That little weenie deserved to know who was paying him back. Just desserts. That's all.

Bill: Yeah, well. You should have thought about just desserts for me and Miranda, not to mention yourself and your future.

Ariel: Great. That's just great. (*She slumps in self pity.*) That's what I get for trying to be helpful.

Miranda: (*She enters from the back room and looks around.*) Who were you talking to?

Bill: Myself.

Miranda: Oh. Are you okay? You haven't been acting your normal self lately.

Bill: (*Tired*) Oh, yeah? Well, times aren't normal, Miranda. What do you expect? Watch the shop for me? I think I owe Mary a visit at The Mariner.

Miranda: Sure.

(*Freddie enters, looks at Miranda.*)

Freddie: Hi.

Miranda: Hi, Freddie. What are *you* doing here?

Freddie: I thought I'd take my favorite song bird to lunch, if she's not too busy. Whadya say?

Miranda: Oh, I can't. I told Bill I'd watch the shop while he goes over to The Mariner to . . . . take care of some business.

Freddie: The Mariner? I'd stay away from there if I were you. That place is weird, and I would definitely not order oysters on the half shell. How about some take out? I'll pick something up and we can have a picnic right here.

Bill: (*He grabs his coat.*) Enjoy your lunch. I'm off.

Freddie: Bye. Nice to see you again.

Miranda: Good luck. (*Bill exits.*) How about sandwiches and coffee. The café next door is pretty good. I'll have their veggie special.

Freddie: You got it. Be right back.

Miranda: Great. Thanks, Freddie. (*He exits and Miranda sets up the chess board stage left.*)

Ariel: (*Talking to the two spirits around her.*) I'm glad somebody around here's happy. Bill and his brother won't speak to each other. The Mariner is probably going to make Bill pay for the mess I caused. Even Cal is fed up with me. I'm a failure, an idiot, a worthless human being doomed to wander in the wasteland forever. And besides that, nobody likes me. (*Slumping again*) Unless . . . . (*Sitting up in a moment of drama*) . . . . unless I make moral restitution for the wrongs I've committed. (*Normal voice resumes. She crosses to center.*) Ooh, this could be good! (*She turns and talks to the spirits.*) Who does that leave? Freddie and Miranda, King and Queen of Happiness. (*All three run to the shelf for a book of spells and throw the book on the floor center stage as all three frantically search for something.*) Ah-ha! Here it is. This is the one. "Love at First Sight." Hmmm. I wonder if it's retroactive. Never mind. It'll have to do. This is my last chance for doing a good deed. Let freedom ring!

Curtain

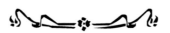

Scene 3: *It is five o'clock in the afternoon. Cal is at the register waiting on customers. Miranda and Freddie are drinking coffee and playing chess down left. Ariel and her spirit friends are watching them, almost hovering at times to make sure everything goes as planned.*

Freddie: Are you sure you won't go with me to the concert tonight? I'm leaving tomorrow and I'm not sure when I'll see you again.

Miranda: I'm sorry, Freddie. I promised Shane.

Freddie: You know, I hate to admit it, but that's what I like about you. You're so . . . . nice. I mean, I'd love for you to break the date and go with me, but if I were in that guy's shoes, I wouldn't think much of you if you did.

Miranda: You make me sound like a saint.

Freddie: You are. Saint Miranda. You couldn't be wicked if you tried.

Miranda: I can be wicked.

Freddie: I'd like to see that.

Miranda: Oh, really? Well, close your eyes.

Freddie: How can I see if I close my eyes?

Miranda: Do you want to see Saint Miranda's wicked side, or not?

Freddie: Okay, okay. (*He closes his eyes and Miranda kisses him on the cheek. He keeps his eyes shut and smiles.*) If I keep my eyes closed, can I see it again?

Miranda: No. That's enough wickedness for now.

Freddie: (*He opens his eyes and takes Miranda's hand.*) You couldn't possibly be really wicked. (*He kisses her hand.*) You're an angel. (*Ariel smugly smiles and signs a thumbs up.*)

Ariel: (*She crosses to Cal.*) Isn't that sweet. If my freedom weren't in the balance, I might puke. I can't believe what love makes people say to each other. At least if something goes right for Miranda, and Bill thinks I had something to do with it, he'll release me. I need outa here! I'm suffocating.

Cal: (*In a soft tone, almost a whisper*) How do you know they didn't fall for each other without your help? What makes you think *you* should get the credit?

Ariel: Oh, just wait. It's not over yet. (*She points to the phone, which rings. Cal looks stunned.*) Answer it.

Cal: (*He picks up the phone.*) Tempest—magic and books. May I help you? Oh, Miranda? Sure, hold on. It's for you.

Miranda: (*She crosses to Cal and takes the receiver.*) Hello? Oh, hi, Shane. Oh, no. You're calling from the emergency room? What happened? Oh, no. How? Oh, I'm so sorry. No, no. It's okay. Really. Don't worry, I'm fine. No, that's okay. Go ahead and give the tickets to your brother. No, really. I don't mind. I hope you feel better soon. Okay. I'll check on you tomorrow, okay? Yeah, me, too. Bye. (*She puts the phone down and turns to Cal and Freddie.*) Shane was working the lunch shift at The Mariner and a waiter came through the door too quickly with his tray. Shane fell down two steps and broke his ankle. He can't go tonight.

Ariel: (*Looking at Cal*) See?

Freddie: The Mariner? Again? Maybe you should stay away from that place altogether.

Cal: (*In a low tone*) You made him break his ankle? What kind of a person are you?

Ariel: A desperate one. Besides, it'll turn out okay. It's not really broken, just sprained. (*Cal shakes his head in disbelief.*)

Freddie: I hate to sound too grateful in the face of tragedy, but does that mean you're free tonight?

Miranda: Yes, I guess it does.

Freddie: Listen, do you really want to go to the concert tonight? I found a quiet little Italian café on my way over that has a cozy table for two with some of those drippy candles and soft music.

Miranda: Sounds nice, and I would hate to go to the concert without Shane.

Freddie: Then it's settled. No concert without Shane. Definitely no concert. Shall we dine tonight, my angel? (*He helps her put her coat on, pulls on his, and they exit.*)

Cal: I guess you're gonna tell me that was all your doing?

Ariel: Of course, it was, silly boy. Am I good or what?

Cal: I have one question. What makes you think you know anything about love and who's supposed to be together?

Ariel: I know more than you do, that's for sure.

Cal: Don't think for even one second that you know me. You know nothing about my personal life.

Ariel: Okay, then where's your girlfriend? Where are all the girls you can even call *friends*? Huh? Show me one who's crossed this threshold. Show me one, period.

Cal: I WORK here. I leave my personal life at home where it belongs.

Ariel: You're always *here* when you're not at school. I see things the way they are.

Cal: What is this, the Inquisition? Why do you care, anyway?

Ariel: I don't. (*She picks up a rubber ball and begins tossing it to her friends, back and forth among the three of them, keeping it away from Cal.*)

Cal: Then lay off, okay. Maybe I don't want a girlfriend.

Ariel: Oh, I get it . . . .

Cal: No, you don't. I like girls. But it's none of your business.

Ariel: Okay, so you just don't want to be bothered.

Cal: I just don't want to be bothered by girls like you.

Ariel: (*Taken aback.*) What does that have anything to do with anything?

Cal: Look, I like you, when you're not hitting me or poking me with something.

Ariel: I'm just playing with you.

Cal: Yeah, well, you're okay most of the time other than that.

Ariel: Aren't you the least bit curious about what I look like?

Cal: Not especially. You have an okay voice and your sense of humor's . . . . different. It's really not bad. Except when you're making fun of me.

Ariel: I'm just kidding.

Cal: I appreciate the way you're ruthless and passionate about life. And I like the way you never give up.

Ariel: Ha! Now you really don't know what you're talking about.

Cal: Yes, I do. More than you know. I'm actually going to miss you. (*He catches the ball and puts it back on the display.*)

Ariel: Okay, don't get all emo on me. (*She heads for the back room.*) At the rate I'm going, (*She parts the beaded curtain and looks back at him.*) I may never leave this place.

Curtain

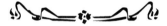

Scene 4: *It is Sunday morning. The shop is closed. Bill unlocks the door and Mary, the manager of The Mariner, follows him in.*

Mary: Thanks for breakfast, Bill. It was a nice change to eat somewhere without fish on the menu.

Bill: I enjoyed it, too, and I'm glad we had a chance to talk about Friday night. Be sure and send me a bill for any other expenses.

Mary: I will, if necessary, but I don't think you have to worry. Mr. King settled everything with our accountant.

Bill: I'm gonna make some coffee. Can you stay?

Mary: Sure, I think I can spare a few more minutes away from the disaster area. (*Bill crosses to the back room.*) I love what you've done with the shop. I haven't been here since your Dad—

Bill: (*Poking his head through the beaded curtain*) You what?

Mary: The shop looks great, Bill.

Bill: Oh, thanks. Miranda gets all the credit. (*He steps back in.*)

Mary: I love this whole street full of shops, especially this one. I've lived on this island all my life. I'm not sure I could ever leave it. (*Bill re-enters.*) When I was a little girl, my mother made me a velvet cape and dressed me up like a little Victorian girl for the Christmas festival. I still have the pictures.

Bill: We moved to the island from the mainland when my father bought this shop. It was his dream. He'd been working as a tax accountant for a big oil company—hardly ever saw his wife and kids. One day he packed us all up and moved us here. I'll never forget his excitement when he unlocked the door and gave us a tour. That was ten years ago. And here I am, still trying to make his dream come true.

Mary: Is this shop your dream, too?

(*The door opens and Miranda enters, followed by Freddie, Anthony, Vince King, and Gonzales.*)

Miranda: Hi, Mary. Bill, Freddie asked me to meet him for breakfast with everyone. I thought you might want to say goodbye. (*An awkward silence fills the room.*)

Anthony: (*He steps forward, glancing quickly at Miranda as he confronts Bill.*) I . . . . owe you an apology.

Bill: No, I was wrong. I've been so wired lately and . . . . (*Anthony grabs Bill and puts his arms around him as the brothers reunite.*)

Anthony: I think we owe this happy reunion to Freddie and Miranda. They've become good friends, very good friends by the look of it. I can't believe how much she's changed in three years. She's not a little girl any more.

Bill: (*He shakes hands with Vince and Gonzales.*) Just made coffee. Miranda, can you find some more mugs?

Ariel: (*She gets up from the chair and talks to the air.*) What does he mean, "Owe it to Miranda and Freddie?" They wouldn't be together if it weren't for my magic. (*She crosses down center with the spirits.*)

Bill: (*He crosses to Ariel down center.*) I guess this is goodbye. (*He offers his hand.*)

Ariel: (*Stunned but elated*) You mean, I can go? I'm free? (*Bill nods and Ariel hugs him. She rushes to the door, slowing as she approaches it and pausing before she opens the door and exits. She does not look back. The two spirits remain and wave goodbye.*)

(*Miranda enters with a tray of mugs of coffee, which she begins offering to the group.*)

Vince: Bill, I have a proposition for you. Come back with us to LA for a visit, as my guest. Bring Miranda. The three of you deserve some time together. While Miranda's out there, if you like, we can schedule an audition. I'll arrange it with some of my people. What do you say? We can leave today—no time like the present.

Bill: I don't know. (*Anthony and Miranda step forward, his arm around her.*)

Miranda: Bill, please.

Bill: Well, I guess I'm outnumbered. What about the shop?

Miranda: Cal can take over for a couple of weeks, Bill. He's responsible and now that the festival's over, things will slow down a bit. He knows everything about running the shop.

Mary: Bill, I could come by every day and check on Cal, if that would help.

Bill: Mary, I couldn't ask you to do that.

Mary: It's done. That's what friends do. I'd be happy to.

Bill: Thank you. For everything. I owe you dinner when I get back.

Vince: Great! That settles it. I'll get my secretary to make arrangements right away. (*He pulls out his cell phone and crosses left.*)

Freddie: I guess this means today isn't our last day together.

Miranda: No, I guess not. (*She looks at her brother.*) I'm so happy, Freddie. Thank you. (*They cross to the chess table down left to sit and talk.*)

Anthony: (*He turns to Bill and Gonzales.*) You've done well with the shop.

Bill: Thanks. Miranda's the inspiration.

Anthony: I never saw the point before. I mean, when Dad moved us here and took over a magic shop, I thought he'd lost his mind. I understand now. (*He looks around the shop.*) More than ever. What happened today was a miracle—like magic.

Bill: That's the most profound thing I've ever heard you say.

Anthony: (*He lifts his mug.*) To magic. (*The others offer the same toast, "To magic."*)

Curtain

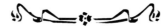

Scene 5: *It is Monday morning. Cal unlocks the shop door, turns on the light, hangs up his coat, and goes into the back room to make coffee. Clatter can be heard from the back, when the door opens again. A girl about sixteen years old enters and looks around the shop, touching things gently as if remembering something. It is Ariel, but a slightly different Ariel, a bit more conservative and settled somehow. The spirits see her, rush over to her but she can no longer see them. They look at one another and move slowly back into a corner.*

Cal: Oh, may I help you? I didn't hear you come in.

Ariel: I saw your "Help Wanted" sign in the door and thought I'd come in. Have you filled the position yet?

Cal: No, I haven't actually. Would you like an application? The owner and his family are in LA for a couple of weeks. I'm in charge now. I'm Cal . . . . Hey, do I know you? Your voice . . . . I feel like we've met. Have you been in the shop before? What's your name?

Ariel: A . . . . Alice. I'm new here. I've just returned after being gone a long time, a really long time. Thought I'd try to get used to the place again by getting a job. So, here I am.

Cal: Yeah. Good idea. Here's an application.

Ariel: Thanks. Do you mind if I sit here and fill it out?

Cal: No, not at all. Hey, would you like some . . . . tea? All I have is chai, but it's really not bad. Kinda spicy.

Ariel: It's so cold out. That'd be great. (*He crosses to the beaded curtain. Several ladies enter and begin looking at books. Ariel watches. One picks up the book of spells on a table down center and shows her friend in audible gasps. Cal returns.*) I'd be careful with that one. I hear those spells really work. (*The ladies giggle and take it to the register, reaching into their purses to buy it. Cal glances at "Alice" with his mouth open in surprise, hands her a cup of tea, and goes to the register.*)

Cal: Let's see. That will be nineteen seventy five. Thanks very much. Come back soon. We'll have another shipment of books on Thursday. (*He hands the lady her package.*)

Lady: Oh, we will! (*All three ladies exit giggling.*)

Cal: (*He crosses to "Alice."*) How did you know?

Ariel: Let's just say I've had a little experience with magic. (*She hands him the application.*)

Cal: You're hired. Can you start today?

Ariel: Yes. Yes, I can.

Cal: Hey, look, can you show me some of the other good books on spells? I'm afraid I have more experience stocking the shelves than reading what's on them.

Ariel: (*They turn to the book shelf to look.*) Actually, this one is my favorite.

Cal: Wait. I wanna make a list. (*He grabs a tablet and pen.*)

Ariel: Here, let me. (*She grabs the paper. The old Ariel is back.*) Okay, now you're going to need . . . . (*Cal leans back on the counter and smiles.*)

Cal: (*Picking up the ball from the display*) Here, catch. (*Ariel turns around slowly and smiles at him, catching the ball he has tossed.*)

Curtain

Games

Rose and Allie are cousins whose fathers' conflict with each other has caused a rift in the family. The cousins, also best friends, avoid their fathers' hostilities by escaping to the family camp on the lake, with Rose's brother Tee in tow, after school ends. Before leaving, Rose meets the newest love of her life, and Allie tries to convince her he isn't good enough. This new love interest, Orlando, shows up at the lake, too, working as a delivery boy for Adams General Store, the girls' major source of supplies during their stay at the camp. Looking like a river rat, Rose is unable to face him when he makes a delivery, and she spontaneously disguises herself as a boy before answering the door. It is in this disguise as "Roy," a twin brother she invents on the spot, that she decides to continue to meet him until the last scene of the play. The characters pass the time playing board games, but these aren't the only games they play. Rose, dressed as Roy, decides to play tricks with Orlando's sensitivities before revealing the part she is really playing. After all, Shakespeare's Jacques reminds us that, "All the world's a stage and all the men and women merely players." Each character in "Games" has issues that must be addressed as they seek equilibrium on their journey into and through the teen years. It is not coincidental that the necessary renewal and cleansing take place in a back-to-nature setting. In *As You Like It*, on which "Games" is based, the characters of Rosalind, Celia, Orlando, and Oliver resolve their differences and disguises in the Forest of Arden, a place of refuge where wounds can heal more easily. So it is with the camp on the lake surrounded by a forest where Rose, Allie, Tee, Orlando, and Oliver must come to terms with who they are and where they're going—at least for the summer.

Synopsis of Scenes

The action of the play takes place in four locations: at the home of Cecil Adams, grandfather to Orlando, Oliver, and Phoebe; at the gym at St. Stephen High School; outside the dormitory at St. Ann's School for Girls; and at the Wolfe's summer fishing camp on the river.

Act I
Scene 1: Mid morning in the living room of Orlando's grandfather, Cecil Adams
Scene 2: That evening at a wrestling match at St. Stephen's
Scene 3: Three weeks later outside the dormitory at St. Ann's
Scene 4: Next morning at "Duke" Wolfe's fishing camp on the river
Scene 5: That evening a little after ten inside the cabin
Scene 6: The next night in the cabin

Act II
Scene 1: Next morning, outside the front of the cabin
Scene 2: That afternoon outside the cabin
Scene 3: That evening outside the cabin
Scene 4: That night at the party under the stars outside the cabin

Characters:
Orlando Adams: graduating senior at St. Stephen High School
Cecil Adams: Grandfather to Orlando, Oliver, and Phoebe and owner of Adams General Store on the river
Gloria: Oliver's girlfriend
Oliver Adams: Orlando's older brother and small business owner
Two wrestlers at St. Stephen's
Referee at the wrestling match at St. Stephen's

Allie Wolfe: Graduating senior of St. Ann's and Rose's cousin and friend
Rose Wolfe: Graduating senior of St. Ann's and Allie's cousin and friend
Frederick Wolfe: Allie's father
Thomas "Tee" Wolfe: Rose's twelve year old brother
Phoebe Adams: Eleven year old sister of Orlando and Oliver
Mr. Corin: Long time friend of the Wolfe family with a cabin nearby
Audrey: Corin's daughter and a junior in high school
Roy "Duke" Wolfe: Rose's father who has recently been fired from his
　　　job by his own brother Frederick

ACT I

SCENE 1

Orlando, a senior at St. Stephen High School, is sitting in his grandfather's house with his sister Phoebe. They have just come from the reading of their father's will.

Orlando: (*He is visibly upset.*) Grandpa, I don't understand how this happened. How could Dad leave everything to Oliver and nothing for me to go to college? What was he thinking?

Grandfather:　I'm sorry, son. I don't know. He *wasn't* thinking. He was in so much pain toward the end. No one gave a thought about his will. People do strange things when they're sick. He had to have believed at some point that Oliver would take care of whatever you needed for college. He was a good man, your dad. He wouldn't have abandoned your education. Son, I'm sorry. If Oliver doesn't come around, the best I can offer you is a job working as one of our delivery boys. You can start next week, if you're ready.

Orlando: Thanks, Grandpa. I dunno. It's bad enough to lose Dad, but to be betrayed by your own brother, too. I guess I just need some time to think about it.

(*Oliver enters with a girl by his side. They are laughing and talking until he sees his brother and grandfather looking glum.*)

Oliver: Hey, what's up? Why so serious? (*Orlando glances sharply at him. His grandfather puts his hand on his shoulder.*) You look terrible. Hey, Gramps. This is Gloria.

Gloria: Hi, everybody. (*She flashes a smile.*)

Grandfather: How do you do, young lady.

Oliver: Gramps, you gotta see my new wheels. Me and Gloria picked up my new truck this afternoon.

Grandpa: That's fine, son. I'm happy for you. (*Phoebe gets up, walks out, and slams the door behind her.*) Well, I reckon I'd better be getting back to the store. (*He looks at Orlando.*) We'll talk later. (*He exits.*)

Orlando: Oliver, you and I need to talk *now.*

Oliver: I'm busy. (*He grabs Gloria.*) Besides, there's nothing to talk about.

Orlando: How am I supposed to pay for tuition now?

Oliver: Look, man, that's not my problem. Get a job like the rest of us.

Orlando: You know Dad intended for that insurance money to help pay for my education, too. (*The anger in his voice is rising.*)

Oliver: Look, little brother. When are you going to get it through your thick skull? If Dad had wanted you to go to college, he would have made provisions. He didn't. As it turned out, he invested it in my business long before he got sick. Maybe he thought it would pan out sooner than it did, but it just didn't, okay. So quit your bellyaching and get over it. I'm sick of hearing it. (*He hands him some cash.*) In fact, when are you moving out?

Orlando: Now wouldn't be soon enough for me. (*He exits.*)

Curtain

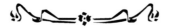

SCENE 2

The scene opens at a wrestling match hosted by St. Stephen High School, a Catholic day school for boys. Rose and Allie, two girls who are about to graduate from the boys' sister school, St. Ann's, sit in the front row. They are clearly not avid sports fans, but it is obvious that Rose has taken an interest in one of the wrestlers.

Allie: I can't believe you dragged me here. I hate violence.

Rose: Sh-sh-sh. They're getting ready to start.

Allie: Just remember what a good friend I am. You owe me.

Rose: Look, Allie! There he is! Oh, be still my beating heart.

Allie: He's a day student. He doesn't even board here.

Tee: Okay, now exactly who is this guy?

Rose: He's here on a wrestling scholarship. He lives with his grandfather.

Tee: I bet he gets to eat whatever he wants.

Rose: I have to do this now. It could be my only chance.

(Rose watches the two boys get ready to make their moves. The referee blows the whistle and the match begins. The two contestants engage in the typical moves, Rose groaning and cringing until one is pinned to the floor. The ref swings his arm close to the floor three times and the game is over. The boy Rose has been watching intently has won the match. The loser gets up and walks off the mat. Rose has risen to her feet. She looks at the boy who has won, and he notices the girl standing near him staring adoringly. He is also entranced. She walks over to him and hands him what seems to be a locket on a chain.)

Allie: What is she doing?

Tee: *(From aside he talks to Rose.)* You'll never get a date. Did you brush your teeth?

    (Neither can speak. The referee breaks the spell by rushing him off the mat for the beginning of a new match. The boy begins to walk away but looks back at Rose. He is somewhat bewildered by the unexpected surge of feeling. Allie is still sitting with her arms crossed over her chest looking a little annoyed at her friend.)

Allie: What are you doing! *(They exit, Allie pushing Rose and Tee toward the door.)*

Orlando: *(Two of his teammates gather around him.)* Who *was* that girl? Oh-h. Why couldn't I say anything to her? I'm doomed to silence. Stupid, stupid silence. She thinks I'm an idiot now. *(He hangs his head in shame.)*

Curtain

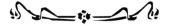

SCENE 3

The scene opens outside the dormitory at St. Ann's with boxes and luggage stacked and ready to go. It is the final day of life on campus and the girls have packed to go home for the summer. The luggage belongs to graduating seniors Rose and Allie Wolfe, whose fathers Frederick and Roy "Duke" Wolfe are brothers. It is late evening and Rose and Allie recall the day's events. Rose is upset.

Allie: If you want to give a total stranger the locket your mother left you, who am I to interfere?

Rose: You really don't understand. But then, how could you? You have it all. And if you don't have it, you go shopping. (*Allie looks hurt and shocked at her best friend.*)

Allie: We're going to college, Rosie. We've waited so long for this day. Just think about it. College! Freedom. College men. You can't let a hometown boy you hardly know interfere and change all your plans at this point. You have to forget him and move on. He's a little fish and you've got to throw him back in. Consider him a . . . . distraction, that's all.

Rose: Distraction, huh? I never thought of people you care about in such a callous way. It's funny, Allie. I graduated with honors and I got the scholarships I really wanted, and everything fell into place just like that. I know how lucky I am, but it's not enough. I feel so . . . . sad. Our dads parted ways with harsh words, and now, I don't know what's going to happen to my dad or me, or even Tee. Your father virtually forced Dad out of the business. He's officially in the ranks of the unemployed, not to mention the fact that our fathers aren't speaking to each other. Maybe we should stop speaking, too.

Allie: (*Stunned*) No, you're right. But Dad must be going through some kind of midlife crisis. He's out of his mind. Even Mom won't talk to him.

Rose: If you're worried, don't be. My dad is a trooper. He'll go to the camp on the river, regroup, and come back strong. He and your dad may be brothers, but they're as different as night and day. After he's communed with nature a while and figured out what to do, he'll be back in business.

Allie: Yeah. I'm sure you're right. You are about almost everything. (*Changing her tone*) I just don't want you to waste your time with a day student.

Rose: (*Pulling away*) Okay. So why *don't* you like Orlando?

Allie: Have you made plans to be together?

Rose: No.

Allie: Has he ever called you?

Rose: No.

Allie: Has he climbed mountains, traversed the countryside, forded rivers to see you? (*She doesn't comment but looks could kill. Allie pays no attention to her glare.*) Sent flowers? Letters? Gifts?

Rose: No! No. He hasn't but . . . . look, Allie.

Allie: What are you doing? You're usually so serious. Are you playing games?

Rose: You know me better than anyone else, but maybe there's one thing you don't know about me.

Allie: Uh, oh. You're not going to tell me you're really a serial killer, are you? (*Making fun of her*) You don't have this dark side with a monster about to rear its ugly head at me, do you?

Rose: (*She finally smiles.*) Allie! Get serious. Are you listening? (*She hesitates.*) Now don't laugh. (*Taking a deep breath*) I believe in the laws of attraction.

Allie: That's it? What's so unique about that? Everybody believes in attraction. Birds and bees. Peanut butter and jelly. Ham and eggs. Things go together.

Rose: Hmmm. It's a little more complicated than that. I'm talking about . . . . about . . . . calling the things you really want into your consciousness.

Allie: What? Rose, are you on something? You're starting to scare me. Too much stress. That's it. You've been under a lot of strain lately with graduation and your dad and all—

Rose: Say what you will. I don't believe in coincidence anymore. Things happen for a reason, and when you believe good things can happen to you and you allow them to happen, a cycle is created—

Allie: Wait a minute! Wait a minute, I get it. You've been watching that movie again. (*She begins to dig around in one of the boxes near their luggage.*) The one with the name I can never remember. (*Rose doesn't answer.*) You know, the one with John Cusack and he keeps looking for that girl's telephone number in this book that he's supposed to find at a resale shop. What was the name of that movie?

Rose: (*Mumbling, almost inaudibly without looking at Allie*) Serendipity.

Allie: What was it?

Rose: (*Quietly*) Serendipity. It was *Serendipity.*

Allie: Oh, yeah. That's the one. You really need to lose that movie, and fast. (*Rose starts to protest.*) That was fiction. You live in the real world. I'm not so sure about all this calling stuff into your life, Rosie. Don't you think that maybe you did well in school because you just worked hard? And *then* everything else fell into place? You got what you deserved—you earned it!

Rose: Do you think that's what happens? You think everybody gets what they deserve?

Allie: Honey, I NEVER get everything I deserve, but that's another story. You, on the other hand, deserve to get what you want. You never ask for much, and when you do, you've always earned it.

Rose: (*Pauses*) I want Orlando. Whether I deserve him or not, he's my soul mate. I saw it in his eyes. When he spoke. It's meant to be.

Allie: When he *spoke?* Neither one of you said a word.

Rose: We spoke with our eyes.

Allie: With your eyes. (*Looking at her watch*) Would you look at the time! Dad is picking us up any minute now. Are you ready? I can't wait to get to the penthouse! I'll get a different nail color every day. I heard that Justin Bieber moved in next door.

Rose: Allie, I can't go home with you for the summer.

Allie: When did you decide this!

Rose: I didn't. Your dad doesn't want anything to do with mine. After this weekend, I don't know where fate is taking me.

Allie: You . . . . don't . . . . want to meet Justin Bieber?

Rose: Allie—(*She hesitates, preparing to make an announcement.*) What if we both spent our summer vacation at the camp? You could come with me. Just think about how much fun we could have. Fishing and swimming in the river, canoeing, sitting under the stars talking about our dreams.

Allie: I'd rather sit *with* the stars, *living* my dream. Besides, not even Justin would go there. Rose, uh, thanks, sweetie, but I am the quintessential city girl. If it isn't chlorinated and if I can't see my pedicure through the water, this girl's not going in.

Rose: Okay, then canoeing!

Allie: Too much work.

Rose: Well, what about all those yummy cookouts? S'mores . . . . hot dogs . . . .

Allie: I'm dieting. Anyway, have you ever looked at the ingredients on a package of hot dogs? It makes me shudder to think what part of an animal is stuffed into one of those little casings. (*Rose gives her the do-we-really-have-to-talk-about-this look.*) Besides, too many insects. All those hairy legs and wings buzzing around—they make my skin crawl.

Rose: Yeah, maybe you're right. I'll miss you.

Allie: Well, I guess we'll drop you off at your place.

(*Allie's father Frederick Wolfe enters. He has come to take his daughter home.*)

Fred: (*He makes a point of not looking at his niece Rose.*) How's my girl?

Allie: Hi, Dad. We're all ready to go. Let's put my things in first so Rose can get hers out more easily. We're taking her home. Uncle Duke can't pick her up.

Rose: Hi, Uncle Fred.

Fred: (*He speaks as if Rose isn't present.*) Rose isn't coming. We don't have room. Besides, we aren't going home just yet.

Allie: (*She puts a box down sharply.*) What? What do you mean Rose isn't coming? Of course we have room.

Fred: She isn't coming with us. That's all.

Allie: Dad, Rose is standing right in front of you. We're her family. We have to help her.

Fred: Not anymore. As far as I'm concerned, I don't have a brother and I don't have a niece.

Allie: Dad! What are you saying? You can't do this to us. To me!

Fred: I can and I will. Now pick up the boxes and let's load up the car. I have a meeting in three hours. We're cutting it close as it is.

Allie: (*She turns to Rose who is now sitting on a trunk. Both are bewildered.*) Rose . . . . I . . . . Rosie . . . . I'm sorry. I don't know what to say. I'm so sorry. I don't know what's come over him.

Rose: It's alright. I should've expected this. I did wonder how Uncle Fred was going to treat me after everything that's happened between him and Dad. I was just hoping we could make it past this whole leaving school business. I'll call a taxi. (*She takes out her cell phone.*)

Allie: No. We'll both call a taxi. When my dad comes back for me and the last of the luggage, I won't be here. Come on. Help me take your things out back. By the time he finishes loading mine, we'll both be out the back. We'll run away like Shakespearean heroines. Will that general store take my credit card?

Curtain

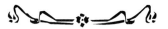

SCENE 4

The scene opens in a rustic camp on the river in a cozy family room. The look is definitely wood with remnants of hunting and fishing, yet lived in comfort with books and photographs and old, and probably dusty, knickknacks placed around the room. Rose and Allie look around and reminisce. They're in jeans and T-shirts, looking sleepy and somewhat disheveled. It is mid morning. Rose picks up a baseball cap, dusts it off a bit, and puts it on, stuffing her hair up under it.

Allie: I'm jumping in the shower. I feel like a river rat already and we've been here one night. (*Picking at her hair*) What is this grunge in my hair? Does your dad keep cleaning supplies around?

Rose: Uh, yeah, (*She seems distracted.*) bottom cabinet in the kitchen, or bathroom or, not sure. Dunno. (*Allie leaves.*)

Allie: (*Calling from another room*) By the way, did you know there's a baby lobster out back. He's crawling out of a little hill of mud.

Rose: (*Yelling back*) It's called a crawfish. People around here eat them.

Allie: (*She pokes her head back through the doorway.*) Ew. Raw?

Rose: No, silly. They boil them first.

Allie: They eat their eyes?

Rose: Go take a shower. (*Allie turns around mumbling the word "disgusting."*)

Rose: (*The camp phone rings.*) Hello. Oh, hi, Dad. Yeah, Tee's here. Sorry, my cell phone died. I decided to come to the camp for the summer. Allie's here, too. (*Pauses*) Oh. Uh-huh, uh-huh. Yeah. How did you know I'd be here? Oh, yeah, that's right. No, I didn't forget. Okay. What? You won't be here till Friday? That's a whole week away! Okay, okay. Yes, I want you to get the job. Right . . . . right . . . . right. Yeah. I love you, too. Okay. Bye.

(Tee is rummaging through the fridge when a knock at the door is heard. He jumps up to see who it is.)

Tee: It's your boyfriend.

(Rose sees him through the window, panics, and opens the closet looking for a place to hide. An avalanche of hunting and fishing clothes and gear come tumbling over her. She grabs a jacket, hat, sunglasses, and a fishing pole before grabbing Tee and stuffing him in the closet.)

Rose: You make one sound and I'll take your iPad.

Orlando: Mr. Wolfe? Delivery from Adams General Store. (*He knocks again.*)

(Rose looks out the window and steps back inhaling audibly, a look of panic spread across her face. She pulls the cap down on her forehead before opening the door.)

Rose: (*Opening the door and taking the first box from Orlando, she lowers the pitch of her voice.*) Hey, Dad's not here right now. I'll sign for that. Man of the house, you know.

Orlando: Hey, I didn't know Mr. Wolfe had a son. Are you here for the whole summer?

Rose: Yeah, he's got a son and a daughter. Uh, twins. And a younger son, too. But his daughter's not here right now. They'll be here later. I'm just getting stuff ready for the women . . . . and . . . . children . . . . when they come here . . . . soon.

Orlando: Oh, okay. (*Perplexed at the sight, he looks back at his order form.*) Well, I think that's about it. No, wait. Lemme go back to the truck. There should be one more. (*He exits.*)

(*Rose paces frantically, mumbling to herself, and grabs the box of fishing lures.*)

Orlando: (*Returning*) Wow, you're really into fishing, huh.

Rose: Yeah. You know what they say. Teach a man to fish . . . .

Orlando: Right. Hey, I think my Grandpa missed a box. Okay if I bring it tomorrow?

Rose: (*Feigning a calm demeanor again, picking up the lures and examining them.*) Yeah, sure, whatever. See ya.

Orlando: Okay, man. Check you later. (*Rose closes the door almost pushing him out.*)

Rose: (*She sighs and takes her cap off, falling onto the couch grinning. There is another knock at the door. She runs to an interior door calling for Allie's help.*) Allie! What are you doing in there? I need you out here NOW, (*No answer, just the sound of water.*) Oh-h-h! (*Rose hears a knock at the door. She runs to the window and remembers Tee in the closet. She opens the door.*) Oh, sorry I left you in the closet. You scared me. I thought you were someone else.

Tee: Got anything to eat? What are you doing with Dad's hunting gear on? Can I have my hat, please. (*He pulls a bag of chips out the delivery box, looks at Rose for approval.*)

Rose: Be my guest.

Tee: Are you playing games again? Girls are so strange.

Rose: (*Ignoring his question*) Allie's in the shower, where, I might add, she's been for the past twenty-five minutes. I had to face the delivery boy by myself.

Tee: What's wrong with that? Boxes too heavy?

Rose: Tee, it was Orlando at the door. I had to pretend to be my brother so he wouldn't see me looking like a grunge.

Tee: You pretended to be *me*?

Rose: My twin brother. I couldn't let him think that this was me. I just met the guy. Our relationship can't be over before it gets a respectable beginning.

Tee: You don't have a twin brother.

Rose: Shut up. Maybe you were adopted.

Tee: You're a psycho.

Rose: It's all part of the plan.

Tee: Okay, whatever. Got some cards?

Rose: There should be cards and games in this chest. (*She opens it and begins looking for cards.*) Oh, wow. I haven't seen these things in so long. Look, *Snakes and Ladders*. I used to play this with Dad for hours. (*She hauls it out and sets it on the table.*)

Tee: What and what?

Rose: You know, the board game. *Snakes and Ladders.*

Tee: (*He looks at it.*) Oh. Vipers in *Candy Land*. Cool. Let's play. Got anything to drink? (*Allie emerges in a cute outfit, looking like she just stepped out of a teen fashion magazine, starkly out of place in a camp on the river. Tee and Rose stare at her.*)

Allie: You wouldn't believe how long it took for the hot water to kick in. Hey, Tee.

Tee: Hello. Where are you going in that get-up? Wanna play *Snakes and Ladders*? It's interactive multi-user.

Rose: Really? You want to play? Great! (*She begins setting up the board.*) I love that game.

Allie: Play what?

Rose: Don't you remember playing this when we were younger? Actually, Tee, I don't think you weren't around yet. C'mon, guys, it's a classic. You throw the dice and move the number you get. If you land on a snake, you go back to the beginning. Land on a ladder and you advance. Like life, sort of. (*They both look at her at the same time.*)

Allie: When was the last time you stepped on a snake? Come to think of it, I've never seen you on a ladder either?

Rose: Come on, Allie. It's symbolic. Or metaphoric. (*Serious now, she pauses to think.*) Or both. You know, I read once that everything in life is a metaphor. If that's true, all symbols must be metaphors, too. That means snakes and ladders could be both symbolic and metaphoric, don't you think?

Allie and Tee: Who cares!

Tee: Let's just play. I'm on a winning streak. By the way, what do I win? (*He continues to play games on his iPad and eat.*)

Allie: What makes you think you're gonna win. I might win, you know.

Rose: No, I'm gonna win. (*She picks up the phone and calls Adams General Store.*) Adams General Store? Is Orlando there? (*She pauses.*) Hey, Orlando. (*She coughs.*) Nah, just had some crud in my throat. You know that extra box of food? We're going to be playing games later and wondered if you could bring it over tonight. If you don't have to work, maybe you could join us? (*She listens.*) Pizza? Yeah, sure. Man fuel.

Allie: So, he's on his way over here. It might be a good idea if you go and change, right?

Rose: Things are falling into place just like I knew they would. Sometimes destiny needs a little help.

Tee: Why do girls feel they have to create these elaborate schemes to get a guy? You already confuse us most of the time without even trying. Besides, don't you know all you really have to do is feed us and throw a little attention our way every now and then?

Allie: What would you know about girls?

Rose: You know, I could have sworn there was a monopoly game up there. (*She pulls a ladder over and climbs up to look.*)

Tee: Oh, look. The snake's on the ladder. (*Allie and Rose turn to stare him down.*) What? It's symbolic.

Curtain

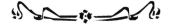

Scene 5

Tee and Rose are playing Monopoly *on the floor in front of the couch on which Allie is sleeping. It is later in the evening, a little after ten.*

Tee: Okay. Give me six hotels on Park Place. (*Rose looks at him with disbelief.*) What? I can cover it, and in about ten minutes, you're goin' belly up, baby.

Rose: (*Yawning*) Go ahead. I'm almost there. (*She yawns, stretching, and falls over pretending to be an insect with legs in the air.*) Look, I'm a roach. Belly up. (*Recreating the dying twitch*)

Allie: (*It isn't clear if she is awake or talking in her sleep.*) Roach? Where? (*She sits up and then goes back to sleep.*)

There is a soft knock at the door. Tee gets up. Rose quickly stands up, looking around for the cap, and Allie remains in a semi-fetal position, undisturbed by the interruption.

Tee: I'll get that. (*He looks out the window.*) Okay. Are you ready? It's your guy. (*He throws her the cap.*) And he's got food. Yes! This is one cool dude.

Rose: (*She grabs Tee's arm.*) Wait! I lied. I can't do it. I'm not ready for this. Don't let him in. I've changed my mind!

Tee: Too late. Food's here. Destiny is knocking. (*He opens the door as Rose quickly dons the cap.*) Hey, man. Thanks for coming over tonight. I'm Thomas, but everybody calls me Tee.

Orlando: Sorry it's so late. I was gonna wait till morning but I told my grandfather you'd probably be up and—(*He looks at Allie.*) Hmm, I guess not everybody's awake.

Tee: Yeah, but that's okay. More food for us, and I'm starving. All right! Cheetos, Pringles, Oreos, pizza. This is the stuff. You're a genius. (*He takes the boxes and starts rummaging through them.*)

Orlando: So, are you guys here for the summer?

Tee: (*Still looking in the box*) Nah, I'm just hanging out for a couple of days before I go to computer camp. Rose and Allie are.

Orlando: What about your friend over there? (*He points toward Rose and then speaks to her.*) I'm sorry. I didn't get your name. (*Rose is looking at lures in the box of fishing tackle, her cap pulled down over her forehead. She looks at Tee blankly.*)

Tee: Oh, that's Ro . . . . Roy, Rose's brother. Twin brother. I think you met earlier.

Orlando: (*He looks around the room, spots a framed photo of Rose and her dad.*) Oh, yeah. Hey, who is this girl? I saw her at my match the other day. (*He picks up the photo and studies it.*) What's it doing here?

Rose: (*She glances at Tee, then lowers her pitch, still not making eye contact with Orlando.*) Sister. (*She puts a stick of gum in her mouth and starts chewing and talking at the same time.*) That's my sister Rose. Twin sister.

Orlando: Rose? Rose. This (*He points to the girl in the photo.*) is your sister? (*Rose nods. Orlando is dumbfounded, baffled but smiling at his good fortune. He holds the photo to him but Rose pries it out of his hands and returns it to the shelf.*)

Tee: (*Jumping in*) Yeah. Hard to tell, though, lookin' at Roy. But yes. (*Putting his arm around Rose's shoulder*) Fraternal.

Orlando: Right. Fraternal. (*Laughing and wondering at Tee's joke*) So where is she? Rose, what a beautiful name. For a beautiful girl. I only saw her once, but I couldn't take my eyes off her. In fact, she was standing right in front of me and I couldn't even say anything. I blew it. She probably thinks I'm an idiot. (*Tee laughs.*)

Rose: You said nothing? What happened?

Orlando: I just stood there, frozen. And then you know what she did?

Rose: What?

Orlando: (*He pulls from around his neck, under his shirt, a chain with a circular charm attached to it. Rose slowly slumps in a chair downright looking at Orlando.*) She gave me this. She said, "Wear this for me. For luck." And then she walked away. Actually, I think a friend of hers dragged her away.

Tee: Yes, that would have been Sleeping Beauty here. Orlando, meet Allie. This is her best side. (*Tee points to her back side, laughing.*)

Orlando: I really don't remember much about it, but I do know this. I couldn't take my eyes off Rose. Hey, listen, maybe I could write her a note and when she gets back you could give it to her for me.

Rose: Sure, man. Here. Write on this. (*She hands him some paper. Orlando starts to scribble something, thinks a moment, and writes again.*)

Orlando: Hey, thanks. (*He folds up the paper and hands it to Rose.*) I think I'm in love.

Rose: Hmm. Okay, whatever. (*There is an awkward moment of silence.*) Hey, look. Rose might be back by tomorrow night.

(*Rose hits Tee who is about to speak.*) Why don't you stop by and we can all chill—eat, watch a movie, play cards.

Orlando: Great. I usually finish deliveries around seven. I'll clean up and come over about eight. (*He stops and turns around.*) Oh, wait. I'm sorry. I told my grandfather I'd take my sister Phoebe to a movie tomorrow.

Rose: Bring her, too.

Tee: That is, if she doesn't mind an exciting evening of *Monopoly* and *Snakes and Ladders*.

Orlando: Snakes and ladders?

Tee: You'll see.

Rose: Just come over and bring your sister. The more, the merrier. (*Orlando exits. Rose pulls the cap off and reads the note. After a few seconds, she sighs, "Aw-w-w." Tee grabs the note and begins reading aloud as Rose grabs once at the paper.*)

Tee: "No one knows
How much I love Rose.
I'd come to blows
With anyone who gets between me and my Rose."
(*He is silent then takes a deep breath.*)
This is really bad. Even for you, this seems like a new low.

Rose: Okay, so he needs a little help with his verse. Not everybody is cut out to write poetry. But it's so sweet. Look at it this way. What kind of guy takes the time to write poetry to tell a girl how he feels about her? (*She sits on Allie, forgetting she's on the couch.*) Oops, sorry, Al.

Allie: What? What's happening?

Tee: You missed it. (*He sits on the other side of Allie.*) Orlando's in love with Rose, and he's written her very bad poetry. But Rose is posing as her brother Roy, *which*, of course, Orlando hasn't figured out, *which* could be very interesting. Who said nature was boring? Can I finish off the chips and dip?

Rose and Allie: No! (*They begin pelting him with pillows.*)

Curtain

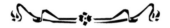

SCENE 6

Rose, Allie, and Tee are getting the games out. Rose has Snakes and Ladders, *Tee has* Monopoly, *and Allie has* Candy Land, *which she stares at, shaking her head.*

Allie: *Candy Land?* I played this, maybe when I was five. You've got to be kidding.

Rose: Orlando's little sister Phoebe might like to play, and she's ten.

Allie: Since when did you become Martha Stewart? (*Rose gives her a warning look.*)

Tee: I know you can't help it. You're a victim of love mush.

Rose: Is that like oatmeal for two?

Tee: With butter and brown sugar? What's for dinner? (*He begins looking for food.*)

Rose: Remember that spinach salad Allie made three hours ago?

Tee: (*He looks up.*) That was dinner? What happened to the meat? Where's the entrée? Where's the man fuel?

Allie: Listen, my little bottomless pit, you wanted to stay here, right? Well, Rose and I have been reading up on veganism. There's a bag of squash, zucchini, cucumbers, tomatoes, lentils and bulgur on the table. (*He frowns.*) Anyway, we're both on a diet and we're not going to lie around gorging ourselves all summer before we go off to college. I'm a size 0 and I plan to stay that way.

Tee: What's *veganism*?

Allie: Well, it's when you eat only—(*There is a knock at the door. Allie opens it.*) Hi. You must be Orlando. And this must be your sister Phoebe. (*They enter slowly. Phoebe spots "Roy" and walks over to her. Rose picks up a decoy and starts showing it to her.*)

Orlando: Hey, thanks for letting us come over tonight. Is Rose here yet? (*Aside to Rose*) Did you give her my note? I've got some more. I've been writing every break I had today, you know, between deliveries. (*He pulls five or six more letters out of his pockets.*)

Rose: Uh, yeah. I mean no, not yet. She's not back yet, but, uh, I'll give them all to her when she, uh, comes back, which could be any day now.

Allie: (*Looking right at Rose and Phoebe and left at Tee and Orlando*) Okay. Right. Terrific. Let's play a game. (*She feigns enthusiasm for Rose's sake.*) Who wants to play *Monopoly*? (*No response.*)

Phoebe: (*Looking at the games on the table*) I wanna play *Candy Land*. I played that when I was five. It was my favorite. Orlando let me win every time.

Orlando: You knew?

Phoebe: I wanna play with Roy. (*She sidles up to Rose.*) The rest of you guys can play *Monopoly.*

Tee: Hey, I've got a better idea. (*He takes control of the situation for Rose's sake.*) Let's let Roy and Orlando play *Snakes and Ladders,* and you and Allie and I can play *Candy Land.* Okay, let's get set up. (*He quickly hands people boxes of games before anyone can object. Rose and Orlando sit down right and the others gather at the table to play Candy Land. Phoebe, who is sulking, looks back at Roy with sad eyes.*)

Orlando: Okay. So what is this game we're playing?

Rose: *Snakes and Ladders.* See, here's how you play. You throw the dice and move your marker the number you get. If you land on a ladder, you jump ahead. But if you get a snake, well, you have to go back. I love this game. It's just like life. Did you have to read that poem by Yeats in English—my senior English teacher loved Yeats—what was the name of it? Anyway, she made us memorize it. (*She recites the lines slowly and seriously as if they mean something to her now.*) "Now that my ladder's gone, I must lie down where all the ladders start, in the foul rag-and-bone shop of the heart." (*Silence. Orlando just stares, as if he has heard something important.*) Kind of like where the snake is. It's how you—

Orlando: I get it. Believe me, I get it. Lately I've been a steady customer in that rag-and-bone shop. Can I tell you something? My life was about to crash until I met your sister.

Rose: Until you met my sister? *Rose?*

Orlando: I don't know if you can understand this, but she didn't even know me when she asked me to wear her necklace for good luck. My dad just died and I can't afford to go to college.

For a minute I thought I was a somebody again. You know, like good could happen again, like fate had something good in store.

Rose: Did you tell her?

Orlando: No, that's the problem. I just stood there like a dork. That's why I've been writing all those poems to her. I know I can't write, and she'll know that when she reads them, but I want her to see I'll do anything for her, even make a fool of myself.

Rose: (*She is somewhat speechless, just staring at him.*) I see. Yeah, well, I think you ought to be straight with her—no love poems, just the plain truth. I mean, the love poems are nice and all, but just talk to her.

Orlando: What if I can't? Last time I tried, nothing would come out.

Rose: Sounds like you need some help. Listen, I know Rose pretty well, right? I mean, you know what they say about twins. Why don't you let me help you. We could practice. I can be Rose and you can be you. How 'bout it?

Orlando: You mean practice? Actually pretend . . . .

Rose: Sure. Come on. We can start now. (*Phoebe interrupts.*)

Phoebe: I don't wanna play this anymore. Orlando, tell us a ghost story, a scary one. He's really good. (*She jumps up.*) Let's turn out the lights.

Orlando: NO. Not tonight, Phoebe. We can do this later when we get home.

Allie: Wait. Orlando. You know some good scary stories? Okay. That's it. Storytime. *Candyland* is over. I'll get the candle.

Orlando: (*Looking at Phoebe*) Did you have to bring this up tonight?

Phoebe: (*Grinning*) Tell the one about the girl named Allie.

Allie: Oh? There's one about me? Even better. (*Allie lights a candle on the coffee table and turns out the lamp. Everyone gathers around, on the couch, chair, floor. Phoebe takes a seat next to Rose.*)

Orlando: Everybody settled? Okay. Here goes. Once there was a girl named Alexandra, and she was the most beautiful girl in the town. (*Allie smiles.*) The only problem was, she knew it (*Allie's smile begins to fade.*) and looked down on everyone else who was not beautiful or handsome. One night while she was sleeping, a spider crept across her face (*Allie softly emits an "Ew".*), stopped for a moment, and then crawled away. The next morning, as every morning, the first thing she did was admire her beautiful face in the mirror. When she looked closer, she noticed a tiny red spot on her cheek. Horrified, she began to panic. She ran downstairs to ask her mother what it was. "It looks like a spider bite. Don't scratch it, and it'll go away in a few days," her mother told her. But as the day went on, the spot grew bigger and bigger, until her mother finally said, "I'll call the doctor in the morning. It looks like it might be infected." By this time, Alexandra looked terrible. She moped and cried and wailed that people would see only the huge boil on her cheek. In tears she asked her mother, "What can I do? I look so ugly!" To which her mother replied, "Take a nice warm bath and you'll feel better." She had been in a tub of water only a few minutes when the boil on her cheek burst—(*His voice gets louder*) and out came hundreds of tiny spiders crawling all over her face—in her nose and mouth and ears. (*He leans over and uses his finger to crawl over Phoebe's face a she grabs Rose and squeals. Rose jumps up.*) She slid under the water to make them stop. Later that evening, Alexandra's mother climbed the stairs to check on her daughter. No sound came from the bathroom. She climbed to the top and called. Still no answer. She opened the door and saw her daughter—under the water, drowned. But crawling out of the tub were hundreds of tiny black spiders.

Allie: Gross! That's disgusting! Anyway, spiders can't swim. Can they? I'm turning the light back on. (*She gets up, turns the light on, and blows out the candle.*)

Phoebe: Oh, I love that one! Didn't you like it, Roy? Let's tell some more!

Allie: I think one's enough. In fact, you know, I think I'm gonna head off to bed now. It's getting late. (*Muttering*) That was so creepy. Ugh.

Orlando: Oh, sure. (*Looking at Allie*) Sorry. I hope I didn't scare you. Phoebe likes 'em scary and I figured . . . .

Allie: Me? Scared? Oh, no, not at all. (*She begins subtly looking for spiders under papers, between books, under cushions.*) Hah! Me, afraid of spiders? Don't be ridiculous. (*She laughs nervously while Tee puts his arm around her and tickles her.*)

Orlando: Well, I guess we'd better go now. (*He grabs Phoebe and they head for the door. He turns around.*) Hey, Roy. Do you wanna go fishing in the morning?

Rose: (*Moving closer to Orlando.*) Yeah, man. Like 9:30? Hey, I was thinking, maybe you could come over and play cards tomorrow night. We could practice what you're going to say to Rose or something.

Orlando: Nine-thirty? You want to leave at 9:30? Okay, yeah, sure. Hey, maybe your sister will be back by then? (*Phoebe pulls on his sleeve and he shrugs her off.*)

Rose: Uh, well, sure. Maybe.

Tee: (*Still standing by Allie, he has retrieved a can of insect spray from her.*) Oh, good. Poker. We'll get a game of poker going. Now you're talking a man's game.

Allie: Oh, you'd like that. Winner takes all?

Tee: Of course.

Allie: Careful. Rose might beat you. She's good at games. (*Rose gives her a look of warning.*)

Orlando: Goodnight, everyone. Thanks for asking us over. It was fun.

Phoebe: Goodnight, Roy. I hope I see you again soon.

Rose: See ya round, Phoebe. (*Aside to Orlando*) We'll practice tomorrow, okay. (*He gives her a nod and then he and Phoebe leave. Rose shuts the door, pulls her cap off and sighs. She runs to the table to pick up her notes from Orlando and opens one.*) "Oh, my love is like a red, red rose. Because my love is Rose." Well, at least he's heard of Robert Burns. "I love my Rose with all my heart, and if she asked, I'd take her to Wal-Mart." Oh, how sweet. He likes to shop. (*She opens another one.*) "Roses are red, violets are blue. With me at her side, Rose'll never be blue."

Allie: He clearly has feelings for you, Rosie, but honestly! His poetry stinks. I'm going to bed. This is way more entertainment than my brain can stand. Besides, I broke a nail. (*Allie exits. Rose follows, opening and reading yet another note. She enters briefly to turn out the light and hand Tee a blanket. She exits again as Tee settles in on the couch. After a moment, Allie enters with a flashlight. She picks up the can of bug spray. Only the light from the flashlight can be seen and the only sound is one long spray of insecticide.*)

Tee: (*Lying on the couch with his eyes closed, he lifts his head.*) What is that smell?

Allie: (*In a wee voice*) What smell?

Tee: Go to bed, Allie. There aren't any spiders in here.

Allie: (*In that same wee voice*) Okay. (*When the flashlight goes out, one more s-s-s-t-t is heard.*)

Curtain

ACT II

SCENE 1

The second act opens the next morning outside the front of the cabin. Allie enters from inside with a hand mirror, looking intently at a spot on her face.

Allie: (*Groans, touching a spot on her cheek that she sees in the mirror, and begins talking softly to herself*) Oh, no. Please, no. Let it be something else. (*Yelling now*) Everyone, get out here, NOW! It's happening! (*She touches what she perceives to be a red spot on her cheek.*) Rose! Tee! Come out here, now! (*No response. She finally notices small white papers tacked to the columns of the cabin as well as the trees on either side.*) What's all this? (*She takes one down and reads it.*)

"I think that I shall never see
A flower as beautiful as my Ros-ie.
A smile so sweet
And skin soft as wheat
I hope when we meet
It will be really neat."
Ug-g-g-h. It is too early for this.

Rose: Mornin'. Everything okay? I thought I heard someone yelling. What are you doing out here? Wait a minute. Are you turning into nature girl? There's hope for you yet.

Allie: Please. This is no time for sarcasm. Besides, you have no idea what you just said. I may be giving birth to nature any minute. Look at my face, Rose.

Rose: (*Looking closely at her face*) What? I don't see anything. Where?

Allie: (*Looking in the mirror and growing frustrated*) Right here! This red blotchy looking boil thing. (*Pointing to a red pin point of a spot*) Here. Don't touch it. Rose, what if it's . . . .

Rose: What if it's . . . . what?

Allie: You know. A . . . . a . . . . oh, my gosh, Rose. I really don't think I'm all that beautiful. (*Close to tears*) Have I really been so vain?

Rose: Oh-h. I see. (*Stifling a laugh*) You think that spot on your cheek is going to get big and puffy and full of little spider eggs and that it's going to pop open and—

Allie: (*She puts her hands over her ears.*) Stop it, Rose! Stop it! Stop it!

Rose: (*She is silent and after a moment Allie takes her hands off her ears. Rose starts singing "Itsy-Bitsy Spider crawled up the window spout . . ." Allie runs into the house and Rose notices a piece of paper on the ground.*) What's this? (*She reads aloud.*) "I think that I shall never see . . . . (*She mumbles the rest and smiles.*) Aw-w-w. (*She then notices the others and runs around taking them down from the posts and trees. A phone rings inside.*)

Allie: Rosie, that's Mr. Adams from the general store. Did you order more food? He said Orlando was on his way over.

Rose: I didn't order anything. It was probably Tee, the bottomless pit.

Tee: (*Enters pulling a tee-shirt on*) Hey, watch it. What's for breakfast?

Allie: Tee, did you order anything from the store?

Tee: Nope, but it's not a bad idea. Wouldn't turn it away if it showed up. Why?

Rose: Mr. Adams called and said Orlando was on his way over.

Tee: (*His gaze turns toward the window.*) And you think food is the reason? His *reason* has about ten seconds to put her cap back on.

Orlando: (*He enters carrying two bags of groceries, cheerfully.*) Hey, everyone. I thought while I was making deliveries out here, I'd drop off my own contribution for the party tonight.

Allie: Party?

Orlando: Yeah. Tee invited me to come over tonight for poker. If it's anything like last night, I'd call that a party. Besides, he said Rose might be back.

Rose: Are you ready to go catch some fish?

Orlando: Sun's pretty hot now, but, hey, why not. I'm ready. Let's go.

Curtain

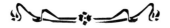

SCENE 2

The scene opens with Orlando and Rose sitting in the boat, their poles in the water.

Orlando: Listen, uh, Roy, we've got some time now. We should practice. I've got this strange feeling I'm gonna see Rose soon. Maybe tonight, and I wanna be ready.

Rose: Oh, right. Okay. Look at me. Now, what would you say to me, right now, if I were Rose? First thing that comes to your mind.

Orlando: (*He closes his eyes and thinks a moment, smiling.*) I'd give her a big kiss. (*Opening his eyes*) I'm not so good with words.

Rose: No. You can't do that. Too fast. It's better to talk first, kiss when you run out of things to say. But, not so fast, buddy. Girls like guys to talk about things first.

Orlando: Oh-h, no, then we'll never get to the kissing part. She's gonna think I'm stupid 'cause only an idiot could be totally speechless with the one he loves.

Rose: Are you afraid of her?

Orlando: No! Well, maybe a little. I don't know.

Rose: What are you afraid of? No one knows her better than I do, and I can tell you she wouldn't hurt a fly. Besides, it's like that play we had to read in English. "Men have died from time to time, and worms have eaten them. But not for love." (*No reaction from Orlando*) Never mind. Okay. Pretend I'm Rose. Now, thank me for coming to your wrestling match and giving you the necklace. Go ahead.

Orlando: Thank you for coming to my match?

Rose: Is that a question?

Orlando: (*He takes a deep breath and tries again.*) Uh, hey, Rose, thanks for coming to my meet and—man, I can't do this.

Rose: Am I your girlfriend or not? What's my name? Look at me. Who am I?

Orlando: (*Barely audible*) Rose.

Rose: Okay, good. Now, what do you want from Rose. Practice on me. Say it now and it'll be easier later.

Orlando: I want Rose to be my girlfriend.

Rose: Okay, I will. At least this week.

Orlando: This week! What are you talking about? I want her to be my girlfriend forever.

Rose: You don't even know me. You'll change your mind in a week. So a week it is.

Orlando: No, I won't. I saw the way she looked at me that day. No one has ever looked at me like that. And the necklace. What do you have to say about that, huh?

Rose: It was just a little trinket, that's all.

Orlando: No, it wasn't. I heard Allie say it had been her mother's necklace.

Rose: (*Changing the subject*) What will you do when I get jealous 'cause you've looked at another girl?

Orlando: I'd say you won't. You're too smart for that. Besides, Rose is the only girl for me.

Rose: (*Dropping her oar in the water*) Oops.

Curtain

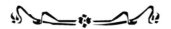

SCENE 3

It is afternoon. Allie, Rose, and Tee are putting up paper lanterns that Orlando delivered for the party. Rose has discarded the "Roy" look and is back to her old self.

Rose: Not there. Let's put this one here. (*She takes the lantern from Tee's hand and holds it up to look at it.*) Oh, look! Little roses. The lanterns have little roses on them. Incredible. And so sweet. I just love this guy. He was so thoughtful to bring decorations and food for the party tonight.

Tee: Whoever heard of decorating with paper lanterns covered with roses for a poker game?

Allie: Sorry, Tee. It's a girl thing.

Tee: Yeah? Well, Orlando's a guy. Not that you can always tell around here.

Allie: I know. Wasn't that thoughtful and sweet. And he's so cute, too, huh, Rosie.

Rose: (*Smiles and nods*) Yes, he is and tonight, he's my guy. Won't he be surprised.

Jim Corin and his daughter Audrey enter. They're staying in the neighboring cabin for the summer and appear to be taking a shortcut from the river after a morning of fishing, from the look of their poles and the fish container Audrey has in her hand.

Rose: Hey, Mr. Corin. Hi, Audrey. How's it going? I haven't seen you guys since last summer.

Corin: Well, I'll be. Is it Rose? You must be a senior in high school now.

Rose: Just graduated in May. I'm getting ready to go to college in the fall.

Corin: Well, congratulations. Audrey here has one more year, and if she can stay away from the boys and study hard enough, she might make it to college.

Audrey: Dad! (*Turning to Rose*) Sorry. He's forgotten what it's like to be in love.

Corin: Ah, it's only a passing whim. What's the point? Love doesn't last because it has no value in our society any more. It's work, hard work, that really matters.

In disbelief or disagreement with Corin's philosophy, the youth keep a sustained silence for a moment.

Tee: (*Entering from the house*) Wow. Look at those rods. Catch something good with 'em?

Audrey: (*Opening the container*) Six large catfish. Big fish fry tonight.

Tee: (*He looks inside, surprised.*) Did *you* catch these, or your dad?

Audrey: Dad got the two smaller ones. I got the rest.

Tee: Impressive. Maybe you could give me a few pointers. I could really dig some fried catfish.

Allie: Careful, Audrey. (*She points to Tee.*) Bottomless pit.

Audrey: (*Ignoring Allie*) Cool. How about tomorrow morning?

Tee: It's a deal.

Audrey: Good. I'll stop by at four-thirty.

Allie: Tee's getting up at four to go fishing? I'll believe it when I see it.

Rose: Mr. Corin, if you and Audrey want to stop by tonight, we're having a little party. Pizza and poker.

Corin: I don't know about Audrey, but I'm beat. You go, Audrey. I think I'll stay close to home tonight. (*Turning to Audrey*) Just be home by 11:30.

Audrey: Dad!

Corin: Aren't you still working on your essay for that correspondence course?

Audrey: No, Dad. I finished that a week ago.

Corin: Well, I guess you can stay till twelve.

Rose: Bye, Mr. Corin. See you tonight, Audrey. (*Corin and Audrey exit. Rose turns to help Tee move a table for the party.*)

(*As Corin and Audrey leave, Oliver enters with his arm in a sling. He has been in a car accident.*)

Allie: Hi. You look lost. Can I help you?

Oliver: Yeah, actually, I think you can. I'm looking for my brother.

Allie: Your brother? What's his name? Is he supposed to be here?

Oliver: Oh, sorry. Orlando Adams. (*Rose turns quickly to look at the newcomer.*)

Allie: Orlando? You mean the guy who's been delivering our groceries from Adams General Store? That Orlando? He's your *brother*?

Oliver: Mr. Adams is my grandfather. Orlando's been working for him. Have you seen him? I really need to talk to him, the sooner the better.

Rose: (*Intervening*) Is anything wrong? Is he okay?

Oliver: I hope so, as soon as I talk to him. We had an argument, sort of, and we need to patch it up. It was probably my fault.

Allie: (*Showing interest*) So, what's *your* name?

Oliver: Oh, I'm Oliver. Adams.

Allie: Hi, nice to meet you Oliver Adams. Sorry I can't help you. (*Attempting to keep him occupied*) But you could use our phone. Or have a coke. Or maybe you could help us put up decorations for the party tonight. (*Looking at the sling on his arm*) Maybe you could just watch. What happened to your arm?

Oliver: I totaled my new car.

Allie: Oh, that's terrible! What kind of car was it?

Oliver: A new red Ford truck.

Allie: O-oh, so you wanta come to our party?

Oliver: Well, I . . . . thanks, anyway. Maybe another time. I really need to get going and find my brother first. I haven't exactly been the best older brother lately. I owe him an apology and I need to set things right between us.

Allie: What changed your mind?

Oliver: It's a long story, but as you can probably guess, it involved a girl . . . . and a new truck. I guess the real reason was a decision my dad made that didn't make life easier for either of us.

Allie: Oh, I understand. My dad's being a real jerk now. Parents just don't get it, but then, you know, they are *human*. They make mistakes just like the rest of us, and I guess it wouldn't hurt to cut 'em a little slack now and then. As for the girl, we're not all femme fatales, you know. Some of us know how to treat a guy, (*moving closer to Oliver*), especially when he's hurt.

Oliver: (*Looking at Allie*) Okay. I'll have to remember that. (*He has forgotten where he was going but snaps back after a moment.*) Better get going now.

Allie: Hey, Oliver. What about tonight? Orlando's going to be here, too. Make up and come to our party, okay?

Oliver: What time?

Allie: Sevenish.

Oliver: We'll see what happens with Orlando.

Allie: Oh, he'll be here. I promise.

Curtain

SCENE 4

It is evening and the outside of the cabin glows with colorful paper lanterns. Food has been brought out on tables and there is a festive atmosphere. Allie and Rose never looked prettier on this warm romantic summer night.

Rose: I love nights like this. The sounds of the crickets, the river lapping the banks, the mockingbirds singing their last songs for the night. It's so perfectly peaceful. What life should be like all the time.

Allie: Hey, as long as we're not talking, OR SINGING about spiders, I'm good. What do you think about Oliver turning up?

Rose: I guess I'm a little surprised. According to Orlando, there was a feud between them, something about Oliver not helping Orlando pay for college. All I know is Orlando was really hurt when he was left out of his father's will. It's bad enough just losing a parent, but feeling betrayed as well had to be really painful. It's difficult.

Allie: But, Rose. There must be some mistake, or at least two sides to this story. Oliver seemed so nice. And eager to patch things up with his brother. He has *suffered*. I mean a broken arm and a totaled truck. (*Muffled phone ringing can be heard.*)

Tee: (*Sticking his head out the door*) Rose, phone's for you. It's Dad. (*He hands Rose a cordless phone.*)

Rose: Dad! Hi, where are you? When are you coming back? (*Pauses*) Tonight? You'll be here tonight? Uh, yes, that's great. Can't wait to see you. Love you, too. Bye. (*She stares at Tee and Allie in silence.*) Dad's coming back . . . .

Allie: We heard. (*She waits for more information.*) He won't be upset if we have a little party, will he?

Rose: No. No, I'm sure he won't. It's just that Orlando is going to be with me tonight, not *Roy*. But I'd like to spend some time with my dad, too. Wow. What timing.

Allie: Rosie, it'll be okay. You have two men who are crazy about you. Enjoy it. I wish it were happening to me. I'd give anything to have my dad pay attention to me and have a boyfriend, too. Things could be a lot worse.

Curtain

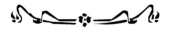

SCENE 5

There's a party going on. Rose, Allie, Tee, Audrey, and Rose's dad Duke are standing around a table laden with food. Glowing lanterns and music create an aura of harmony. Clearly absent from the festivities, however, are Orlando and Oliver.

Tee: (*Audrey and Tee are playing poker, using Oreos for chips.*) Great dip. What'd you put in it? It's got these little black leafy looking things. Whatever it is, it tastes terrific. Okay, Audrey. I'll see you two Oreos and raise you a double stuff.

Allie: Spider legs! (*He stops eating and looks up.*)

Tee: (*He looks up at Rose.*) Did Al just make a joke about insects?

Rose: Progress, huh.

Duke Wolfe: Rosie and Allie, great party. Honey, you're just like your mom. What a cook that woman was. And the place looks so nice. Tidy. I was going to call the exterminator three weeks ago, and I forgot. Hope the bugs didn't get to you.

Rose: No, not at all. Right, Allie? Try these eggplant rolls. Allie and Tee made them.

Frederick Wolfe walks up looking for his daughter. He is about to be confronted by his brother Duke when Allie intercedes.

Allie: Dad!

Frederick: I thought you might be out here. Why didn't you answer your phone?

Allie: All you had to do was call Uncle Duke. He knew where I was.

Frederick: It's time to go home. Get your things.

Duke: Wait, Fred. Can't you see the kids are having a good time? Whatever grief you had with me, leave it there, in the past. For once, let the kids have their fun without having to contend with us. They're innocent in all of this.

Allie: Please, Dad?

Fred: (*He sighs and shakes his head, unhappy but willing to listen.*) What do you suggest?

Duke: For a start, why don't we leave them here and go inside and talk.

Fred: (*He heads for the cabin door.*) Are you going to listen to what I have to say this time?

Duke: (*Smiling as he follows*) Depends on whether I like it or not. (*Both exit.*)

Rose: Well, well. It appears hope abounds on this beautiful evening. Just like calling it into your—

Allie: Don't say it! I know my dad. His bark is much worse than his bite.

Orlando, Oliver, and Phoebe enter.

Orlando: Hi, guys. Sorry we're late. Grandpa needed our help with the new shipment. I want you to meet my brother Oliver.

Allie: Hello, Oliver.

Oliver: Hello, Allie. (*They move over to a table, alone.*)

Orlando: You know each other? (*Neither is listening.*)

Phoebe: Hey, where's Roy?

Rose: He, uh, had to leave . . . . to, uh, pack for camp. He's going to a camp in Arkansas for the rest of the summer.

Phoebe: Oh, man. I really liked him. I made him a list of my favorite songs.

Rose: I'll be glad to give it to him for you.

Orlando: Rose! I've been waiting to see you again.

Rose: Well, here I am.

Orlando: Did you get my letters?

Rose: Yes . . . . all ten of them. You're quite a . . . . (*She searches for the right words.*) prolific writer.

Orlando: Yeah, well. I know I can't write poetry. Look, I'm not good with words. I was hoping you'd get the message anyway. I went into that meet feeling pretty defeated. You changed all that when you gave me your necklace. It was your mother's wasn't it. (*Rose can't speak.*) I guess I need to give it back to you.

Rose: Why? (*Attempting to hide her disappointment*) What do you mean?

Orlando: When I saw you at St. Stephen's that night, I had a feeling I'd see you again. Rose, you're my ladder.

Rose: Your ladder? Like the game . . . .

Orlando: No. The one I've been using to climb out of that sad part of my heart.

Rose: Oh-h. Yeats. You remembered. (*She has realized her slip.*)

Orlando: You know that poem? Your twin brother explained it to me. First time I ever really understood poetry.

Rose: "Now that my ladder's gone, I must lie down where all the ladders start, in the foul rag and bone shop of the heart." So, have you run out of things to say?

Orlando: That's funny. Roy said you would say that—

Rose: Roy?

Orlando: Yeah, you remember. Your twin brother, Roy? (*He takes Tee's cap, moves closer to Rose, and puts the cap on her.*)

Rose: You *knew?*

Orlando: (*Moving closer*) Fish are gone by 9:30, Rose, and what kind of guy drops his oar in the water and says *oops?* (*He leans in to kiss her but is interrupted by Tee who grabs his hat back.*)

Tee: All right! Let's party! (*He takes Audrey's hand and starts dancing. All join in.*)

Curtain

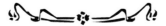

Imogen's War

In 1609, close to the end of Shakespeare's brilliant career, he wrote his last great female role Imogen in the last Romance called *Cymbeline,* and, because Imogen confronts specific moral and social concerns, critics consider *Cymbeline* a "problem play."

Shakespeare found the story of King Cymbeline and pre-Roman Britain in Holinshed's *Chronicles* of 1577 and used it as the basis of his play. Although the wicked queen and her son experience a tragic ending, what one might call just desserts, in the end peace is established between Rome and Britain. All's well that ends well, as the Bard says.

As a spin-off of *Cymbeline*, "Imogen's War" takes place in 1918 in England and France at the end of WW I. General Kimble removes his footman Hugh Post from service in his upper class London home when he learns that his only daughter Imogen has actually married Hugh. The general attempts to have the marriage annulled, but Hugh enlists to fight the Huns and Imogen secretly follows him to the battlefield in France. They both encounter not only the war with Germany but also a war with the people they love.

Throw in some German spies, deception, and the bombing of the French farmhouse and the plot thickens. Just as Cymbeline finally makes peace with Rome, Imogen and her family make amends with each other as the war comes to an end and the Armistice is signed.

Synopsis of Scenes

The action of the play takes place in two locations, the London home of General Linus Kimble and his family and a farm house in northern France during World War I.

Act I
Scene 1: 1918, mid morning in the morning room of General Kimble's home
Scene 2: Next day in the morning room
Scene 3: An abandoned farmhouse on the outskirts of Arras, a little town in northern France.
Scene 4: The same day at the farmhouse.

Act II
Scene 1: The farmhouse the next day
Scene 2: The farmhouse later that day
Scene 3: The farmhouse the same day
Scene 4: Several days later in London at the Kimble home.

Characters:
General Linus Kimble: British general during WW I, father to Imogen, Arthur, and Harold Kimble; husband to Lady Kimble, his second wife
Imogen Kimble: daughter of General Kimble; wife of Hugh Post
Mary: maid
Lady Kimble: wife of General Kimble
Hugh Post: footman in the Kimble household, secretly married to Imogen
Williams: General Kimble's butler
Alice: Welsh lady's maid
Jack Heflin: American soldier spying for Germany
Lt. Brigg: British officer in Arras

Medic: British soldier of the medical corps in Arras
British Soldiers
Mills: a British soldier in the farmhouse, the tea maker
Arthur Kimble: British soldier and son of the General
Private Thomson: British soldier and friend to Arthur
Harold Kimble: Arthur's brother, a soldier who is wounded
Mrs. O'Shaunessy: nurse for the British army
Miss Eliot: nurse serving under O'Shaunessy
Fritz: German POW and spy

ACT I

Scene 1: *The year is 1918 in London. General Linus Kimble, his new wife Lady Kimble, and his daughter Imogen are in the morning room of their home discussing the new production of Shakespeare's* Cymbeline *they saw the night before. Their conversation turns to war. The General is home on brief leave to visit his family and rest. Hugh Post enters. He has worked as a footman for the Kimble family for two years and, before that, as an apprentice doing odd jobs since childhood. He stayed on after both parents succumbed to influenza and went into service at age seven. The General is not aware of the seriousness of the affair his daughter is having with Hugh, believing only that the two have grown up together as brother and sister. His new wife, Imogen's stepmother, has plans of her own for Imogen. To secure the General's inheritance for her own family, she is secretly arranging a marriage between Imogen and her brother's only son Thomas Cloten, III.*

General: Well, I think we can consider the evening a success, wouldn't you say?

Imogen: Oh, quite, if you don't mind an air raid and flickering lights in the middle of the play. But thank you, Father, for the diversion. You did try to make the evening a pleasant one.

General: (*Mary brings in a tray of coffee and pours Lady Kimble a cup.*) Oh, thank you, Mary.

Mary: Will there be anything else, General?

General: No, that's all.

Mary: Very good, sir. (*Exit*)

General: Yes, well the Americans have now entered the war, so the Germans will step up the action on their part. I dare say, at the very least, morale will improve. These Americans are determined to go all the way to Berlin.

Lady Kimble: I think it's all rather boring, this war of yours. Why can't we all just sit down to a nice dinner and forget the Americans and the Germans. It's most inconvenient, if you ask me.

General: Yes, dear. That would indeed be preferable.

Imogen: (*Ignoring her comment*) When do you have to return to France, Father?

General: I looked forward to another week here to finish up some business in London and then go on to Calais, but a letter came today from the War Office. It seems I'm needed on the front as soon as possible. If I can leave tomorrow, I will.

Lady Kimble: Well, then, I suppose I shall make another trip to the country. My brother's having a house party with some quite delicious guests.

Imogen: (*Ignoring Lady Kimble again*) As soon as that? I see.

(*Hugh Post knocks and enters. He works downstairs with the other servants. Imogen has known him well since they were inseparable childhood playmates.*)

Hugh: I'm sorry for the disturbance, General, Lady Kimble, but Mr. Blakely says your car is ready for you, sir.

General: Thank you, Hugh. (*Hugh exits.*) Well, goodbye, dear, (*Kissing her cheek*). I'll be back for dinner tonight.

Lady Kimble: Thomas will be joining us before he returns to the country.

General: Very good. Four is always a good number for dinner.

Imogen: Goodbye, Father. I hope your meeting goes well. (*She gently places his scarf around his neck.*)

General: (*Sighs*) As well as can be expected under the circumstances. Goodbye, dear. (*He turns to Lady Kimble.*) Shall I drop you off at the dressmaker's? The car can wait for you.

Lady Kimble: I suppose I should, but that driver of yours always smells like carbolic. (*Whining*) He's really a most disagreeable little man.

General: (*Sighs*) Yes, dear. I'll speak to him. Are you coming?

Lady Kimble: Oh, all right. (*They both exit. Imogen crosses to the mantle. Hugh re-enters and rushes to her.*)

Hugh: Finally! (*He puts his arms around her waist as she is closing the door. She pushes him away gently.*)

Imogen: No! We mustn't give our secret away, Hugh. Wait a bit longer, at least until Father comes home again. It wouldn't be right for the servants to know about our marriage before we tell Father. He'd never forgive me. You know what happened to Harold and Arthur. Father still isn't speaking to them and even now no one can recall why. Father may not even remember, so you'd better be careful.

Hugh: (*Teasing*) Come on. Give us a kiss. You're a proper wife now. My little wife, the best little wife a man could want. (*He puts his arms around her as the General enters again.*)

General: I forgot my case . . . . what? What's this? Hugh, shouldn't you be downstairs? Imogen, what's going on?

Imogen: Father, please sit down. Hugh and I . . . . must have a word with you, if you can spare a moment.

General: I have a car waiting . . . . What's this about? I don't have time to sit down. Hugh, you must be wanted downstairs. (*Hugh turns to leave.*)

Imogen: Hugh, stay. Father, Hugh and I were married—three days ago—on Saturday in London.

General: That's impossible. You were with your grandmother in . . . . London . . . . three days ago. (*There is a pause as he realizes what he has said.*) Hugh, please leave us.

Imogen: Father, let him stay and hear what you have to say. You might have known this would happen. Our happiest childhood days were spent together. (*She crosses to him and puts her hand on his arm.*) You saw the affection growing between us through the years. I do love him, Father, and he loves me, too. I can't see ever loving anyone as much as I love Hugh. Please try to understand.

Hugh: General Kimble, sir, we—

General: Stop. That's quite enough. I won't be persuaded in this manner by a servant. You're both too young to understand and live with the consequences of such a connection. We'll have it annulled. (*He turns to Hugh.*) Meanwhile, you have two weeks' notice to find a position in another household. (*Hugh looks at Imogen and then exits.*)

Imogen: Father, please. What are you saying? You can't do this. We're married. How can you do this to Hugh? Surely you remember what you promised his parents, both loyal servants to this family until they died.

General: What on earth made you behave so absurdly? Marrying below your station? Everything I've done for you has prepared you to marry a man who could afford to take proper care of you.

Imogen: How very ironic. You see before you a man who is honest and loyal to you, one whom I've come to know and trust. Even you developed a fondness for Hugh. You must have known that my feelings for him would continue to grow. Forgive me, Father, but you seem to think that dismissing people is the way to cope with those who oppose you. (*He is silent.*) You would like to be free of those who would disobey you. (*She crosses to door.*) I suppose you wouldn't mind being free of me.

General: Where are you going?

Imogen: I don't know, Father. Perhaps the country needs more helping hands.

General: Don't be foolish. Sit down here, now, and drink your coffee. (*She pauses, looking at him, opens the door and leaves.*)

Curtain

Scene 2: *It is the next day in the morning room. Imogen is setting up photographs of two young men on the mantle. Estranged from their father, the two men and their portraits have been removed from sight. Imogen replaces their photographs in defiance, or*

perhaps to call them back into a once happy life together. The General and Lady Kimble enter.

Lady Kimble: Of course, *Thomas* is available. And he does stand to inherit quite a large fortune. Think of it, Linus. Don't play the fool this time. Besides, it wouldn't hurt you to have her married off—

General: (*He sees Imogen, crosses to mantle, takes the photographs down and puts them in a drawer of the library table center right.*) I specifically asked that these be taken away. What *is* the matter with you? Why are you defying me?

Lady Kimble: If you'll excuse me, I believe I have some letters to write. (*She exits.*)

Imogen: I have two brothers that I love and miss more each day. I didn't send them away! You leave me little choice, Father. I have married Hugh and we would like your blessing.

General: That's out of the question. I've spoken to Edward and he's arranging for an annulment now. I'm leaving for France within the hour. A car is being brought around. I suggest you cooperate with the solicitor. Let's just put all this behind us, shall we.

Imogen: Yes, you would like that. Goodbye, Father. I won't be here when you return.

General: Don't be ridiculous. I'll see you in a few weeks. Goodbye. (*He looks at Imogen who says nothing. He exits. Imogen puts the photographs back on the mantle. There is a short pause before Hugh quickly opens the door, steps inside the room and closes the door quietly.*)

Imogen: Hugh! Did Father see you?

Hugh: No, of course not. I waited until he left. (*They embrace.*)

Imogen: Oh, Hugh. What are we going to do now? (*She steps back to look at him.*) What are you doing in that uniform?

Hugh: I've enlisted. I'm going to France today. Going to fight the Huns. I can't stay here.

Imogen: No. Hugh, you can't go.

Hugh: I'll be all right. When I come back, I'll get a job and we'll find a little flat and live happily ever after.

Imogen: (*Sitting*) What have I done! So many men have been killed and wounded. I've sent you to a dreadful end.

Hugh: Cheer up! They can shoot at me all they want. No one's going to kill me. I'll be back before you know it. Besides, the Americans landed last week. The war's going to be over before Christmas.

Imogen: Has the treaty been signed yet?

Hugh: No, 'course it hasn't. You know that. I wouldn't have enlisted if it had.

Imogen: Have the Germans surrendered?

Hugh: Surrendered? Have you gone barmy? (*Laughing*) They're more determined than ever. If the Brits and the French are tired of fighting, the Americans make up for it with fresh resolve.

Imogen: One battle—that's all it takes to destroy all my happiness.

Hugh: (*Serious now*) I have to do my bit. I'm available for service now that I'm no longer employed. I have a duty.

Imogen: I love you for your loyalty and (*angry now*) I hate you for your loyalty—to King and country, for the sacrifice we both will make for it.

Hugh: (*Comforting her*) My dearest little wife, I love you for the fuss you make over me. I promise I will come back to you. I have every reason to dodge those Hun bullets. (*He playfully dodges make-believe bullets.*) Here. Give us a kiss (*He pulls her toward him and she smiles*), and take this as my pledge that I will return. (*He fastens a bracelet around her wrist.*)

Imogen: It's lovely, Hugh. It was your mother's, wasn't it. Wait. You—you must have something of mine. Here, take this ring. (*She removes a ring from her right finger and he puts it on his own hand.*) Wear this ring as my pledge to love you always. It will remind you of your promise to me. (*He kisses her hand and they embrace. He breaks away and exits quickly. Imogen sinks into a chair as if she has lost the battle. Suddenly she sits up, crosses to a shelf and pulls out a book with a map. She opens it, scanning for a particular place, looks at it, and hearing a sound, closes the book abruptly. The butler enters with a tea tray.*) Thank you, Williams. Set it here, please

Williams: As you wish, Miss. (*He sets the tray on a table near the sofa and starts to pour.*)

Imogen: I'll see to it. (*He turns to leave.*) Oh, Williams, do you know where Father's old uniforms are kept? I might be needing one or two.

Williams: Why, yes, Miss Imogen. I'll have Alice bring them up later. Would you like them in here?

Imogen: Yes, thank you, Williams. That's fine. Would it be possible to have them sent up this morning?

Williams: Yes, Miss, I believe so.

Imogen: Good. Thank you. That will be all. Ah, one more thing. Williams, could you ask Alice to come up at once, please.

Williams: Certainly, Miss Imogen. (*He bows slightly and exits.*)

Imogen: (*She looks at the map again, then looks up.*) My darling, Hugh. I will see you sooner than you thought possible. (*She opens a closet and removes a military jacket. Alice, Imogen's Welsh lady's maid, enters.*) Alice, Mr. Williams is going to have some of my father's old uniforms sent up this morning. I was wondering if you could take them in for me.

Alice: Take them in? What d'you mean, mum, take them in?

Imogen: (*She tries on the coat and tugs at the neck.*) This one's a bit stiff—(*Glancing at Alice*)—ish.

Alice: Mum?

Imogen: Uh, well, you see, Alice, I'm going to a party—a costume party, and I thought I would go as . . . . my father.

Alice: (*Doubting*) Miss Imogen, you're going to a party as your father?

Imogen: Yes. Can you do it?

Alice: Well, I suppose so. How soon will you be needing them, mum? (*Mary enters carrying a coat and a pair of trousers.*)

Mary: Will you require more, Miss Imogen?

Imogen: Yes, thank you, Mary, perhaps one or two. That's good. You can put them right here. (*Mary sets them on the sofa. Imogen looks at Alice.*) Can we begin now? (*She tries on the coat. It is too big for her and the sleeves hang over her fingers. Alice laughs and then catches herself.*) What?

Alice: Well, Miss. You do look funny with your coat hanging over your fingers. (*Laughing*) You look like a wee girl, mum.

Imogen: Yes, well, we'll soon fix that. Here, I want the length of these sleeves taken up. As for the trousers, we'll go to my room and you can take the measurements you need. I must have these as quickly as possible if I'm to reach Hugh in time. (*She turns sharply to Alice, suddenly realizing what she has revealed.*)

Alice: (*Teasing*) Miss, are you going to fight the Huns in France?

Imogen: Oh, Alice, you mustn't breathe a word. Hugh has enlisted and is leaving for France today. I must see him before he is swallowed up by this dreadful war.

Alice: Pardon me, mum. I don't mean to be nosy, but do you not think it might be a wee bit dangerous? And what will your father say?

Imogen: That's the point, Alice. He of all people must not know. Can you keep a secret? It's of the utmost importance. You mustn't tell anyone, especially Father.

Alice: Oh, I hope you know what you're doing. I don't want to be sending you to your doom. (*She pauses and looks at Imogen's pleading face.*) All right.

Imogen: Then you'll do it? And you'll keep my secret?

Alice: The saints be with me, I will. (*She crosses herself.*)

Imogen: Oh, thanks most awfully. You're an angel.

Alice: You'll be needing one.

Curtain

Scene 3: *The scene opens in a farmhouse in northern France. Imogen has made her way to the outskirts of Arras and has come upon an abandoned farmhouse. Believing it to be unoccupied, she has taken shelter here. For the time, she will hide and devise a strategy to find Hugh. She discovers upon entering, however, that she is not alone. A wounded American soldier, Private Jack Heflin, occupies a dimly lit corner of the room. Startled, she runs for the door.*

Heflin: Wait! Don't go. You're British, aren't you? I'm an American—the only one left out of my company. We were ambushed. The shelling was something awful.

Imogen: You're injured.

Heflin: Yeah, just a scratch. (*He moves his arm and writhes in pain.*)

Imogen: Can I . . . . help? (*She moves closer to him.*)

Heflin: So, what are you doin' here by yourself? Did you get shelled, too? Anybody left besides you?

Imogen: (*Lowering her voice*) Uh, no. I've been wandering around for a while. Must have been in shock. Where am I? I saw a sign pointing to the town of Arras. Is that close to the Somme?

Heflin: Close to the Somme? Not quite. You're north of the Somme, on a farm outside the town of Arras. Front's moved south to the Argonne. Say, what's your name? I knew a guy who wore a uniform like that when he came in, but he was a major. You seem kinda young for that.

Imogen: Looks can be deceiving. Where were you attacked? How long did it take you to find this place? Where were—

Heflin: Can't say how long I've been here. Came under attack two, maybe three days ago. Just been waiting for help.

Imogen: What's your name?

Heflin: Jack Heflin . . . . sir. What's your?

Imogen: May I take a look at that shoulder? I might be able to assist you. (*She moves closer.*)

Heflin: Sure, why not. (*She moves even closer. He pulls off her cap, and her hair tumbles down, revealing a woman.*) Well, well. The Major is a girl. I thought there was something different about you. Who are you? Are you a . . . . spy?

Imogen: (*Pulling her cap back on*) Good Lord, no. My name is Imogen. I'm . . . . looking for my husband. I needed a disguise. It was the only way I could get through. You won't give me away, will you?

Heflin: (*Looking around*) Nobody here to tell.

Imogen: There are no certainties in this war. Anyone at any time could step through that door. I must find Hugh.

Heflin: Naw, I'm not gonna give you away. But, what makes you think you'll find your husband in all this confusion? Do you know what it's like out there? Men dying every day on the field and in the trenches. In fact, there were a couple o' Brits passing through this morning looking for the rest of their regiment. Said everybody in their trench was hit pretty hard. One was hurt so bad his buddy had to carry him. They sat down and rested for a while and then moved on. Can't recall their names now, but . . . . wha'd you say your husband's name was?

Imogen: I didn't. Hugh. His name is Hugh. He gave me this bracelet and promised to return to me, soon. We were married only three days when he left. That was weeks ago. My father drove him to enlist.

Heflin: Well, ma'am. I don't like saying this, but I think he could've been your Hugh. He was suffering but he talked about a pretty wife back in England that he didn't think he'd ever see again. He was hurt pretty bad—arm was practically shot off.

Imogen: No, don't. I'm sure you're mistaken.

Heflin: You're right. Musta been somebody else. (*Neither speaks for a moment.*) I was half outa my mind with pain. (*Silence*) Yeah. It was somebody else. That's right. Coulda been any young Brit with a wife back home. Right?

Imogen: Did he . . . . say anything else?

Heflin: The one wounded so bad? Yeah, he talked a little about his home. Said he had just gotten married. Sounded real sad. Said he was never gonna see her again. Talked about the tokens they had exchanged before he was forced to enlist. (*Imogen releases an audible sob.*) Hey, didn't mean to make you cry. It probably wasn't him.

Imogen: Do you remember what he said his name was?

Heflin: Sorry. Can't say. It probably wasn't your Hugh. (*Silence*) That's really something, you following him all the way to France with a war going on.

Imogen: Yes, well. (*She hesitates, collecting herself.*) You see, my war is with my father, the General. I'm afraid the tactics he uses to command the men who serve under him closely resemble the way he manages his family, (q*uietly, almost under her breath*) even though he seems to avoid actually being in the company of his men. I doubt he's ever really been in a trench. My two brothers, Mr. Heflin, refused to be overpowered by him and disobeyed him, to which he responded by promptly disowning them. I remained the loyal, loving daughter. When Hugh and I married, he refused to take it seriously and quickly dismissed Hugh. It was hardly an issue with my father. He found it quite easy sending a servant away, especially one who had the audacity to marry his only daughter.

Heflin: Why? This Hugh must have done something terrible.

Imogen: Oh, it wasn't what he did. No one could have been more honest and sincere than Hugh. A more loyal footman my father never had.

Heflin: Footman, eh?

Imogen: Oh. It's not what you think. Hugh's parents were both in service for the Kimble household. The epidemic that took my mother was the same that ended the life of Hugh's mother first and later his father, too.

Heflin: Their kid?

Imogen: Out of loyalty and pity, my father took their only child under his protection.

Heflin: The old man doesn't sound too bad.

Imogen: He spared Hugh a miserable life in an orphanage. My father was so kind and good in those days. This war has hardened his heart.

Heflin: Yeah. The Great War. Nothin' great about one lot trying to kill off the other—people you've never met before and have no cause to hate. It makes all of us go mad at times. (*Silence*) So you've known this Hugh for a long time.

Imogen: Yes. We grew up together in blissful childhood. Cook let us help her in the kitchen, sometimes rewarding us with sugar-butter sandwiches. My father often let me go to the park and picnic with the other servants on special days. Hugh was always there, making me laugh.

Heflin: So why'd the general send him away if he liked him so much?

Imogen: You're an American. You wouldn't understand. The daughter of a general with good family connections doesn't marry a servant downstairs.

Heflin: So what will you do now?

Imogen: I don't know. I hadn't counted on not finding Hugh. I suppose I must return to my father's house in London. I was foolish to think I would find him so easily.

Heflin: Going back to London now? Could I ask you to mail a letter to my buddy back in Winchester? (*He digs in his pocket for an envelope.*) It might get to him faster if you mailed it from London. You can see how things are here.

Imogen: Yes, of course. I suppose it's the least I can do. (*She takes the letter and puts it in her coat pocket.*)

Heflin: I'd be grateful to you if you would, ma'am. There was this pub that we spent some time in and, well, the fella behind the bar was good to me and my pals, that is, those of us that were shipped over together from the States. I wanted to thank him and let him know what happened to the others.

Imogen: The others? What happened—

Heflin: They won't be back to get their caps, if you get my drift.

Imogen: Oh, dear. I am sorry.

Heflin: Yeah. Say, can I ask another favor?

Imogen: Favor?

Heflin: I need your help.

Imogen: How could I possibly be of any help to you? I can hardly help myself right now.

Heflin: I haven't eaten anything in two days and I'm not sure what lies ahead. If I can make my way back to the coast . . . .

Imogen: You want money.

Heflin: Anything would help.

Imogen: I have only what will enable me to return home. I'm very sorry, but I have nothing to give you.

Heflin: Sure you do. What about that bracelet on your arm? If you let me have it, I could barter it, you know, get something to eat for it at the next farm or village.

Imogen: My . . . . (*She touches the bracelet.*) Oh, I couldn't—it may be all I have left—if Hugh really is gone.

Heflin: Sure. I understand. I guess I'd do the same if I was in your shoes.

Imogen: (*Silent a moment*) I want to help you. (*Silence*) Surely you know I would help if I could.

Heflin: Yeah, sure. It's okay.

Imogen: I'm going to leave now. I do wish you the best. (*She walks to the door, pauses, takes off the bracelet, runs back to give it to him, and exits.*)

Curtain

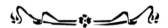

Scene 4: *A British officer enters the farmhouse with several soldiers. The lieutenant glances at Heflin propped up in a corner but continues to direct his men who are apparently moving equipment into the farmhouse. He sends a medic over to Heflin who begins tending to his wound and talking to him. Hugh is in this regiment.*

Lt. Brigg: Private, over here. Set up this phone and let me know when you have contact.

Hugh: Yes, Lieutenant.

Medic: (*Leaving a soldier to tend to Heflin*) Lt. Brigg, sir, the wounded is a soldier from the Ninetieth Division of the AEF. He says he and the others in his company experienced heavy shelling several miles north of this location. He claims he walked for two days before coming upon this farmhouse.

Brigg: The Ninetieth Division, eh?

Medic: Yes, sir.

Brigg: Well, now. I've heard about this infamous Ninetieth Division and their antics in England. All right, I'll see what I can find out from headquarters. In the meantime, move him to field hospital. Post here can assist you. (*Hugh crosses to Heflin.*)

Medic: Yes, sir. (*Turning to Heflin*) Can you walk to the transport vehicle?

Heflin: I think I can manage that.

Hugh: (*Helping him up*) Hey, that bracelet—

Heflin: Oh, that. Yep. There was actually a woman who was here before you fellas showed up. She gave it to me.

Hugh: A woman? Out here? Do you mean a nurse?

Heflin: Nope. At first I thought she was a Tommie, but the more I talked to her I realized there was something different about her. On a hunch I said so and then she took off her cap and confessed. She was looking for her husband, a guy she called Hugh. Thought she'd have an easier time getting through dressed like a soldier.

Hugh: Could it have been my Imogen? Did you say she gave you that bracelet? (*Visibly upset, speaking to himself*) Why would she give up so easily?

Heflin: She believed you were killed in action and didn't want any painful reminders. So she tossed it to me and said she hoped I would get more use out of it than a soldier who wasn't ever coming back.

Hugh: (*In disbelief*) That's not possible. My Imogen wouldn't do that.

Heflin: Here, have a look at it. Maybe it's not you—somebody else. (*Hugh takes the bracelet and examines it.*)

Hugh: (*Reading the engraving*) "To my darling wife Elizabeth."

Heflin: There, *Elizabeth*. See, it must not be your wife. Just a misunderstanding.

Hugh: (*Dejected*) No. Elizabeth was my mother. My father gave this bracelet to my mother when I was born. I gave it to Imogen before I left. (*He slumps down.*) I just don't understand how she could lose faith in me.

Heflin: That's a woman for you. They say they'll wait, but they know what this war is all about. Use it to their advantage, some of em.

Hugh: She gave me this ring. We vowed to each other we would be together again. (*He pauses, looks at the ring, and takes it off. He puts it on the table and exits.*)

Heflin: (*Crosses to door and medic exits in front of him. He is alone for a moment. Heflin pauses, crosses to table, looks at the map, and quickly picks up the ring. He speaks to no one in particular, raising his fist in the air.*) I do this for Germany! (*Exit*)

Curtain

ACT II

Scene 1: *The farmhouse is filled with soldiers, some playing cards, two at the Fuller phone, one entering with a kettle to make tea, several soldiers carrying in supplies. Hugh and the lieutenant and another soldier are leaning over a table looking at a map.*

Lieutenant: Last night a trap was laid in front of British wires at this position (*Pointing to a map*). An enemy patrol must have divided, taken up concealed positions and then opened fire at close range. Three men retreated; one was taken to hospital with a bullet to the chest. We're taking the other two with us. Try to contact base and let them know the details.

Hugh: Yes, sir. (*He begins to use the phone while another soldier looks on.*) It's not making clear contact yet, sir, just static.

Lieutenant: (*Turning to Hugh*) Wait a moment and try it again. Keep trying. (*Hugh takes the phone again. Heflin enters with the lieutenant.*)

Hugh: What are you doing here?

Heflin: My division is 150 miles from here. Until I can join another one, I was told to wait here with you fellas.

Lieutenant: Private Heflin, it would appear, has knowledge of German. The major thought he might be useful. They've captured several Germans and are holding them at headquarters.

Hugh: Oh, right. (*Walks over to Heflin*) So how long will you be here?

Heflin: Couldn't say.

Mills: (*Walking in from the kitchen*) Tea anyone?

Hugh: I wouldn't say no. (*Turning to Heflin*) Would you lads like a cuppa? Mills just put the kettle on.

Heflin: No! No tea . . . . thanks. I don't care if I ever see tea again. No, no tea for me. I've had enough tea for one lifetime.

Hugh: (*Laughs*) I'm afraid that's all we've got. Sounds like you've had a bit of a go with the tea, eh?

Heflin: Oh, I've got a story all right. You see, it was when they put the Ninetieth Division on a British transport to come over here. Me and the rest of the members of my division, we were all in high spirits, ready to drive those Huns all the way to Berlin, but they kept feeding us tea and cheese, tea and cheese until we were sick of it. You see, we weren't accustomed to eating cheese and drinking tea all the time, and we got good and tired of it, I can tell you. Well, when we got to Winchester, we had some time on our own. The men, they all went to town and put on a show. We shot out the lights and kicked up a noise. We demanded something to eat besides cheese and tea. (*He laughs.*)

Hugh: Did you end up in the brig?

Heflin: Oh, it was nothin' like that. When the old man, General Pershing I mean, heard about it, he said to hurry us along to France—he'd give us all the shooting we wanted. We were in bad the day we struck England, but we went to France and did our bit. Anyway, if it's all the same to you, I'd rather not have any more tea and cheese. (*Mills enters with two mugs of tea which he hands to Heflin and Hugh. Hugh takes it and nods. Heflin turns and walks to look at the map. Mills puts the tea on the table untouched.*) So we're right here and the Brits are here? (*Pointing to the map*) What's the plan?

Hugh: Lieutenant thinks we'll be moving those troops down to the Argonne to assist in what could be a new American offensive. He received word this morning that a battalion held out for five days in dense forest until reinforcements arrived. There was shelling all night down there and the Germans came back strong. About half that division was killed or wounded. Huns opened fire at close range and they fought hand to hand . . . . frightful casualties, there were. Not exactly what we'd come for.

Heflin: Is that right. (*He seems entranced by the map.*)

Hugh: Looks like you'll be joining your division here (*He points to the map.*) Good luck to you. (*He picks up a box of equipment and exits. Heflin is alone. He pulls out a small notebook and pen, looks at the map and then looks around before quickly making notes. He puts it back in his jacket pocket as the lieutenant and another soldier enter.*)

Lieutenant: Heflin, it's time. Your transport vehicle is here to take you to the station.

Heflin: (*He sighs.*) It's up the line again for me, boys. Well, let's get goin'. I'm ready. (*They exit.*)

Curtain

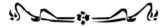

SCENE 2

The farmhouse. A young soldier enters with the lieutenant and another soldier. Several soldiers are sitting around biding time. Hugh is playing cards with his back to the door.

Hugh: (*He turns toward the new men.*) Kimble? (*He crosses to him to get a better look.*)

Arthur: Yes, that's right. Arthur Kimble. (*Moving closer*) Is it Hugh? Yes, I believe it is! My good man! (*Embracing him*) How are you? Out here in the field, are you? What a mess we're in, eh? (*He turns back to Thomson.*) Oh, forgive me. Hugh, this is Private Thomson. We're both part of the 70th. Took some ghastly shelling at the Somme. We're lucky to be alive.

Thomson: How do you do?

Hugh: As well as can be expected. You're safe here. For now, anyway.

Thomson: It's like a dream. I thought I was done for in that trench. When I came to, I was buried under two chaps. Don't know how long we stayed that way, but I think it was the stench that woke me up and I couldn't get out fast enough. That was when I ran into Arthur here.

Arthur: Yes, wasn't that lucky.

Hugh: Yes, well. He's right, you know. Arthur, it's really good to see you. Have you been relocated? What's happening out there? Where's your regiment?

Arthur: I'm lucky to be standing here, Hugh. I was part of a patrol that was barraged with shrapnel for several hours. One of our men crawled back to the lines with a nasty wound to the chest.

Hugh: Well, it's good to see you in one piece without a scratch! Mills actually got a fire out of this old wood stove and provides us with ample cups of tea. Just like home. (*They laugh.*) Just like home . . . . you don't know the news about Imogen and me; everything happened so quickly. We . . . . we're married now.

Arthur: Married? (*Stunned but elated*) Married to Imogen? My dear fellow, when?

Hugh: Yes, married to your lovely sister. Three weeks ago actually.

Arthur: Well, jolly good for you both.

Hugh: It upset the General so much he dismissed me from service. I enlisted the next day.

Arthur: First, old chap, let me offer my sincere congratulations. Not the best of times, but we must grab hold of whatever happiness we can. That doesn't surprise me about Father. Poor Imogen. I'll bet she didn't take his answer well. Did she stand up to the old man?

Hugh: As much as anyone in her position could, I suppose.

Arthur: She's a tough little customer. Still it must have been quite difficult leaving her, especially under the circumstances.

Hugh: Yes. We promised we would see each other again. I'm doing my best to stay out of harm's way, but after all, we are at war.

Arthur: And she meant it. She's a good girl and true. Do you know, I don't think I've seen dear Imogen for two years. Harold's out here, too, you know. Both of us felt terrible about leaving her behind. Father can be quite impossible to live with. But she's really the best. I know she'll be waiting for your return.

Hugh: I'm afraid waiting is not in her character. She was actually here in this farmhouse not long ago.

Arthur: What?

Hugh: That's my Imogen, not one for letting things lie, you know. I take it she got her hands on a uniform, no doubt one of your father's, and tried to pass herself off as an officer. It must have worked because she found her way to this very house.

Arthur: I don't believe it! The silly cow. She's got some pluck, you can say that much.

Hugh: It was vacant at the time, before our company arrived, except for a wounded American soldier whose entire company was lost. He was here for a while, left, and then they brought him back when they discovered he knew a little German.

Arthur: German, eh? Why does this regiment need a translator? Have they taken any prisoners?

Hugh: Not yet, but the lieutenant says to expect several.

Arthur: How interesting. Are you sure? They're usually taken to headquarters. But no matter. I'm sure this is all part of the bigger plan, eh? Tell me more about my sister. How did you find out she had been here?

Hugh: It's odd, really, how everything happened. I still don't understand it all. This American from the 90ᵗʰ Division was wounded in battle and said he found shelter here. Not long after, Imogen apparently came here looking for me and found him. For some reason she decided I wasn't coming back from the war and gave up hope.

Arthur: My dear boy, don't be silly. I'm sure she wouldn't give up hope, not Imogen. Any other woman, perhaps, but not this one. When my sister makes up her mind to do something, nothing can stop her.

Hugh: She gave a stranger the bracelet I gave her. He showed it to me. I read the inscription my father wrote to my mother.

Arthur: (*Sitting down*) I say, I am surprised. There simply must be another side to the story. This certainly does not sound like the Imogen I know.

Hugh: The sister you thought you knew, perhaps.

Arthur: Do you really think so?

Hugh: I don't know what I think any more.

Arthur: How long have you been at this station?

Hugh: Not long. Two days. It's temporary. We're moving out soon. The Americans are gaining ground. There's even talk of an end in sight. (*Suddenly an explosive sound rips through the room as bright red lights flash across the window. Shelling is getting very close. The sound continues and soldiers and medics come bursting in with a stretcher. It is Arthur's older brother Harold.*)

Medic: Make room! (*Medics set the stretcher on the floor. Hugh looks and sees it is Arthur's brother.*)

Hugh: Is he still alive?

Medic: Barely, but he's hanging on.

Hugh: (*Turns and looks at his friend*) Arthur, chum—it's Harold. (*Arthur rushes to his side.*)

Curtain

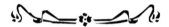

SCENE 3

A young German POW, wounded, has been ushered into the makeshift office, a table and three chairs in the farmhouse. Two nurses, an older matron and a young novice, tend to his wounds. The British officer brings in Heflin and gives him instructions to interrogate the POW in German and to give the translated notes to the officer who leaves them alone. Heflin reveals his identity as a spy to the POW.

Mrs. O'Shaunessy: (*Talking to her assistant and changing the German soldier's bandage*) I need gauze. Quick, girl.

Miss Eliot: Yes, I have it here. Shall I fetch some water?

Mrs. O'Shaunessy: I'll do it. Come here and finish this.

Miss Eliot: (*Trembling*) I've never touched a Hun before.

Mrs. O'Shaunessy: He's a man, just a man. Remember that, my girl. His blood's red, same as yours.

Miss Eliot: Oh, I don't know. He has his jacket on.

Mrs. O'Shaunessy: Well, don't just sit there. Take it off, for pity's sake.

Miss Eliot: (*She begins to reach for his jacket but the man backs away.*) All right, all right. (*Looking at the POW*) I'm not going to hurt you. (*In a low tone*) You dirty Hun.

Mrs. O'Shaunessy: Oh, here, let me do it. You're taking too long. We've got others to tend to, you know.

Lieutenant Brigg enters with Heflin.

Lieutenant: All right, Heflin. See what you can find out. I hope your German is as good as you say it is. When you're finished, Nurse O'Shaunessy needs to change your bandage. Well, I'll leave you to it. (*He exits, leaving Heflin with the German. Heflin looks around to make sure they are alone.*)

Heflin: It's you! Fritz, how did they find you?

Fritz: It was Heinz. He got careless. And greedy.

Heflin: What do you mean?

Fritz: Let's just say his love for money exceeded his love for Germany.

Heflin: What happened?

Fritz: Do you remember the meeting with Schuler?

Heflin: Yeah, so? That was three months ago.

Fritz: The real meeting took place several hours later that night. After you left.

Heflin: Why didn't I know about it?

Fritz: You were no longer needed, my friend.

Heflin: Oh, is that right.

Fritz: Don't be daft. This isn't about you. You gave them what they wanted. That was enough. Heinz went too far. What he didn't know was that he was being set up. Tested, you might say.

Heflin: So where do you come in?

Fritz: Simple. He was passing information to me through a German-American working for intelligence. When things went wrong, he ran; I didn't. Here I am.

Heflin: So they took him out.

Fritz: Yes.

Heflin: What are you going to do?

Fritz: (*Laughing*) Well, my dear friend, it appears that I will not be going anywhere. What do you suggest?

Heflin: I can't help you. I'm risking my own life. What was it you were carrying? Maybe I can make the delivery.

Mrs. O'Shaunessy enters to change Heflin's bandage. Fritz and Heflin begin speaking quietly in German.

Mrs. O'Shaunessy: I'm sorry to disturb you, sir, but now is the best time for me to remove your bandages. If you'll take off your coat, please. (*Heflin removes his coat and a note pad and a small wooden box fall out.*) Uh, excuse me, sir. I must have picked up the wrong gauze. I'll only be a moment. (*She exits with the items in her hand, unseen by Heflin.*)

Heflin: (*Turning back to Fritz*) Time's running out. If you have something, give it to me now or you can forget it. They'll be moving me back to a new regiment soon and it's easier to get letters out here. (*Lieutenant Brigg enters with two soldiers and another officer.*)

Lieutenant: Heflin, come with me. We're putting you under arrest for treason. (*The soldiers move toward him to secure Heflin and take him away. Heflin jumps up and runs for the door.*) Stop him! (*Heflin is met in the doorway by a British soldier who intercepts him.*)

Curtain

SCENE 4

The General has returned from France and is having tea in the morning room with Lady Kimble. The Armistice has been signed and Germany and the Allies are at peace. Williams, the General's butler, enters with letters on a tray.

General: Ah, Williams. The post has arrived. Is there anything for me? Any news from Imogen yet?

Williams: No, sorry, sir. Just a letter for the mistress. (*He hands Lady Kimble the letter.*)

Lady Kimble: Oh, good. I was expecting to hear from my brother. He's giving a party and wants the three of us to join him this weekend. (*She opens and reads letter.*)

Williams: Will you be needing anything else, sir?

General: No, that's all, Williams. Thank you.

Lady Kimble: Linus, I do wish you would stop all this moping and think about the future. A weekend in the country would do you good.

General: We may have signed the Armistice, but I've made a mess of things in this family. My sons have abandoned me and Imogen has run away with my footman. And what's worse—I've been the cause of everything.

Lady Kimble: Nonsense! I say let them all go. Good riddance.

General: (*He looks up sharply.*) What?

Lady Kimble: Well, if your two sons can't obey orders from a general, who will they listen to? As for that daughter of yours, what could she have been up to, running off with a servant? No one will want her now. Young women must think about these things today. She could have had Thomas, you know.

The General turns away from her and looks out the window, shaking his head. The door bursts open and three soldiers enter: Arthur, Hugh, and Imogen still in her disguise with her cap on. The General turns to look and rushes to them before they can speak.

General: You're home! Where's Harold? You've been in France?

Arthur: Father! (*Taking his hand*) Yes, we volunteered with the 70th, the Surrey Regiment—a splendid lot, really. We were stationed mainly near the Somme. But don't worry, Father. Harold is fine but he's in hospital. Took a piece of shrapnel to the leg but he's going to be all right. He's actually back in London. We drove with him in a private ambulance.

General: We must go and see him at once.

Lady Kimble: Linus, what about our weekend in the country?

General: (*Ignoring her, he turns his attention to Hugh.*) Were all of you with the Surrey?

Hugh: No, sir. After you—after I left you that day, General, I enlisted with the 37ᵗʰ, the Hampshire Regiment. I thought if I couldn't do my bit here, I must be needed elsewhere. They were glad to take me, sir.

General: My dear fellow. I was . . . . I was wrong to let you go, but you have served your King and country well. I'm very proud of you. You're good lads. (*He turns to Imogen.*) And you, sir, as well. Let me offer my congratulations and thanks for the courage that all you men showed. We must toast the King. (*He rings for the butler.*)

Imogen: I'm afraid my courage came from love alone, Father. I went to France to find my husband.

General: What's this? Imogen? Is it my daughter? (*She removes her cap and he embraces her.*) And did you find him, dearest Imogen?

Lady Kimble: (*Miffed and annoyed that things have not turned out as she planned*) Well, I can see I'm no longer needed here. I'll be at my brother's, Linus, if you care to join us.

General: (*Speaking only to himself*) Insufferable woman! (*He speaks to Lady Kimble.*) Have a good visit, dear. (*She exits without a reply.*)

Arthur: I believe I have something that needs to be returned, to both Imogen and Hugh. But first, I have quite a story to tell, Father. It seems that we had a spy among us, a man named Jack Heflin, *(Hugh and Imogen gasp at the same time.)* an American of German descent, who was recruited by the Germans to join the American Expeditionary Forces and gather as much intelligence as possible.

General: What? A German spy among your ranks? No! It isn't possible.

Arthur: I'm afraid it is, Father. When he took off his coat to have his bandage changed, a note pad and a little wooden box fell out. The medic examined them before returning the coat, and what do you suppose he found?

General: I haven't the foggiest. Do tell us.

Arthur: In the box were two writing pens and three little vials of liquid, one containing black India ink and the other two—lemon juice!

Hugh: I don't understand. Lemon juice? Did he fancy a bit of lemon squash out there in the trenches? (*He laughs at his little joke.*)

General: Paper, pens, ink, and lemon juice—the tools of a spy reporting information regarding time and place of troops, my dear boy. The spy writes an ordinary looking letter first and then uses lemon juice to write an invisible message between the lines. When the lemon juice dries on the paper, the writing can't be detected.

Hugh: Blimey!

Arthur: Well, when the medic told one of the officers about his discovery, the lieutenant pulled an envelope from his coat pocket. Heflin had asked him to mail a letter to the owner of a pub back in Winchester.

Imogen: (*Looking worried now*) Dear, oh, dear. (*She slowly pulls a letter from the pocket of her coat.*) Did it look like this?

Arthur: (*He takes the letter from Imogen and reads it.*) What's that? Ha! It's addressed to a Mr. Fred Thornton, The Landlord, The Hiker's Rest Public House, Winchester, county of Hampshire.

(*He opens the envelope.*) "Dear Fred, Just letting you know all your buddies shipped out of Southampton the morning after celebrating . . . . la di da di da . . . . thanking you for a good time . . . . in the trenches . . . . Huns unloaded their machine guns . . . ." Looks like the same rubbish as the other letter. (*Turning to Imogen*) Where did you get this?

Imogen: (*Sheepishly*) When Father . . . . when Hugh left for France, I couldn't bear the thought of not going after him. I had a frightful time getting there, but after disguising myself in Father's uniform, which Alice so kindly altered (*She looks at Alice who smiles and nods*), an old man gave me a ride in his wagon to a farm outside of Arras. It looked empty but was actually occupied by an American soldier who was wounded and seemed to be just waiting there, alone. After a brief conversation, he asked me to mail this letter and I agreed. He seemed honest, at the time. But in all the commotion with finding Hugh and Arthur and Harold, I forgot all about it!

Arthur: And he said his name was Jack Heflin? (*He lights a candle.*)

Imogen: Yes, he did. You aren't going to burn it, are you? Isn't that evidence?

Arthur: Hang about a while, my girl. Have a look at this. Do you see it? (*Everyone gathers around the candle to see.*) Can you see the writing that is beginning to appear? Not bad, eh? He's written a secret message between the handwritten lines of black ink. (*As if speaking to Heflin*) It's a bit late for that, old boy.

General: Well done, Imogen.

Arthur: All's well that ends well. Tooteloo, pip pip! Imogen did her part for King and country. (*He embraces his sister who sighs with relief.*) Now for the next bit of good news. The lieutenant who arrested Heflin found something else. You can imagine my surprise when he showed me mother's ring. (*He holds up the ring.*)

General: Good Lord.

Imogen: You have it? You have my ring?

Arthur: (*He hands the ring to Imogen.*) The ring Father gave to you after Mother died? Yes. I won't ask how Heflin came to have it, but it's yours again if you want it.

Imogen: (*With tears in her eyes, she looks at Hugh, who looks away and speaks quietly.*) Thank you, Arthur. Was there . . . . anything else that the lieutenant found?

Arthur: (*He pulls the bracelet out of his pocket.*) Oddly enough, Heflin, in a moment of remorse, said both of these should be returned to the two of you.

Hugh: (*He sighs, relieved.*) My mother's bracelet. Crikey. (*He takes the bracelet.*)

Arthur: I take it you two need a good and proper reunion. Well, go on. (*Hugh and Imogen embrace finally.*)

General: They're right, you know. Forget "stiff upper lip," England, and St. George. Cheers to my Imogen and her Hugh and to love and marriage! Lift your glasses.

All: To love and marriage!

Arthur: And—

General: The King, gentlemen. (*He holds up his glass.*) Peace in our home and our world.

Final Curtain

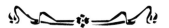

CPSIA information can be obtained at www.ICGtesting.com
Printed in the USA
LVOW07s2121190115

423463LV00001B/433/P